D1445353

ESP

New and future titles in the series include:

Alien Abductions

Angels

The Bermuda Triangle

The Curse of King Tut

ESP

Extinction of the Dinosaurs

Haunted Houses

UFOs

Unicorns

Vampires

Witches

The Mystery Library

ESP

Patricia D. Netzley

Lucent Books, Inc.
P.O. Box 289011, San Diego, California

Library of Congress Cataloging-in-Publication Data

Netzley, Patricia D.
  ESP / by Patricia D. Netzley
    p. cm. — (The mystery library)
Includes bibliographical references and index.
  ISBN 1-56006-770-5 (alk. paper)
  1. Extrasensory perception—Juvenile literature. [1. Extrasensory
perception.] I. Title. II. Mystery library (Lucent Books)
  BF1321 .N48 2001
  133.8—dc21

                                                    00-010094

Contents

Foreword   6

Introduction   8
   What Is ESP?

Chapter One   12
   Telepathy

Chapter Two   27
   Clairvoyance

Chapter Three   42
   Precognition

Chapter Four   57
   How State of Mind Affects ESP

Chapter Five   71
   The ESP-Psychokinesis Connection

Notes   85
For Further Reading   87
Works Consulted   88
Index   90
Picture Credits   95
About the Author   96

Foreword

In Shakespeare's immortal play, *Hamlet*, the young Danish aristocrat Horatio has clearly been astonished and disconcerted by his encounter with a ghost-like apparition on the castle battlements. "There are more things in heaven and earth," his friend Hamlet assures him, "than are dreamt of in your philosophy."

Many people today would readily agree with Hamlet that the world and the vast universe surrounding it are teeming with wonders and oddities that remain largely outside the realm of present human knowledge or understanding. How did the universe begin? What caused the dinosaurs to become extinct? Was the lost continent of Atlantis a real place or merely legendary? Does a monstrous creature lurk beneath the surface of Scotland's Loch Ness? These are only a few of the intriguing questions that remain unanswered, despite the many great strides made by science in recent centuries.

Lucent Books' Mystery Library series is dedicated to exploring these and other perplexing, sometimes bizarre, and often disturbing or frightening wonders. Each volume in the series presents the best-known tales, incidents, and evidence surrounding the topic in question. Also included are the opinions and theories of scientists and other experts who have attempted to unravel and solve the ongoing mystery. And supplementing this information is a fulsome list of sources for further reading, providing the reader with the means to pursue the topic further.

The Mystery Library will satisfy every young reader's fascination for the unexplained. As one of history's greatest scientists, physicist Albert Einstein, put it:

> The most beautiful thing we can experience is the mysterious. It is the source of all true art and science. He to whom this emotion is a stranger, who can no longer wonder and stand rapt in awe, is as good as dead: his eyes are closed.

What Is ESP?

In July 1941 thirty-year-old Dutch housepainter Pieter van der Hurk fell from a ladder and suffered a brain concussion. While in the hospital, he found he was able to predict future events. He received a vision of a neighbor's house on fire, for example, and five days later it burned down. He shook a man's hand and knew instantly that the fellow would soon be murdered; a few days later this vision also came true.

After he left the hospital, Hurk changed his name to Peter Hurkos and began using his new skill professionally. At first he performed in theaters, making predictions for individuals in the audience and telling them personal details about their lives. Then one day he discovered that when he touched an object associated with the victim of a crime or tragedy, he could receive a vision of what happened to that person. For example, when he touched the coat of a murder victim, he "saw" that the victim's stepfather had been the murderer. Sometimes Hurkos also received a vision of a past event without touching anything: after learning about a missing child, he "saw" the girl drowned near a boathouse. Police found the girl at that location.

As he continued to help police and victims' families, Hurkos became famous as a psychic—a person who knows things beyond using the ordinary five senses: taste, touch, sight, sound, and smell. Such a person is said to have extrasensory perception, or ESP—an extra sense that most people either do not have or do not know how to use. The study of psychic phenomena (also known as psi) like ESP is called parapsychology.

Parapsychologists classify ESP into three main categories: telepathy, clairvoyance, and precognition. Telepathy is the ability to send and/or receive thoughts and/or feelings from the mind of another person. Clairvoyance is the ability to "see" events or objects not with the eyes but with the mind. Precognition is the ability to visualize an event before it

Psychic Peter Hurkos used his extrasensory abilities to help police solve crimes.

occurs. Hurkos apparently had all of these skills. When he received information about the people in his audience, he was telepathically hearing their thoughts. When he visualized murder scenes, he was using clairvoyance. And when he made predictions of people's futures, he was using precognition.

Another type of psychic phenomenon is psychokinesis, or PK. Many researchers do not classify PK as a type of ESP, but the two mental abilities are believed to be closely related to one another. Whereas ESP involves the transmission and/or receipt of thoughts, feelings, or mental images, PK is the ability of the mind to directly affect matter. For example, psychic Uri Geller appears to have the ability to bend spoons and start broken watches using his mind alone.

An experiment is set up testing the ESP of twins. The validity of such experiments remains questioned despite continued testing.

PK has been studied since the nineteenth century, as has ESP. But although parapsychologists have amassed a great deal of data on psychic phenomena, they have failed to convince many other scientists that either PK or ESP is real. Skeptics question the validity of parapsychologists' scientific methodology and suggest that most of the information received by psychics could be attributed to lucky guesses. Moreover, objective researchers have had trouble coming up with the same results as ESP testers who believe in the phenomenon. As Mike Dash says in his book *Borderlands*, "Despite many years of hard work and much research, parapsychology has still to produce a viable and repeatable experiment, demonstrating the existence of any variety of psi."[1] When testing conditions are duplicated, the results from one laboratory are not the same as any other—perhaps because of faulty scientific methodology, or perhaps because human beings who exhibit ESP are not consistent in their skills.

But despite the lack of verifiable evidence of ESP, roughly two-thirds of the American public believes in the existence of the phenomenon. According to one study of over fourteen hundred adults chosen at random, 67 percent believe that they themselves have some degree of ESP ability. As Theodore Schick Jr. and Lewis Vaughn report in their book *How to Think About Weird Things:* "Many of us have had experiences that seem to fall into one of [the ESP] categories. We may have thought of a friend moments before she phoned us, or sensed that a loved one was in danger only to find out that he or she actually was, or dreamt about winning a jackpot and then won it. Such experiences appear to be common." However, Schick and Vaughn also note that coincidence and luck could have caused these experiences rather than ESP, saying: "We can't always take our experiences at face value. What seems to be inexplicable often turns out to have a rather mundane explanation. Before we accept the reality of psi phenomena, then, we should be sure that the phenomena in question can't be explained in terms of well-understood processes."[2] In other words, the first step in deciding whether ESP is real involves studying it objectively, considering all possible explanations rather than just the explanation we most desire to be true.

Chapter 1

Telepathy

In 1955 a Wisconsin housewife named Joicey Hurth stayed home while her husband and daughter went to the movies. While washing dishes she had an upsetting experience, as she explains:

> All of a sudden I froze and dropped the plate I was holding. I raised my eyes to heaven and said, "Oh God, don't let her get killed." I just knew something was wrong. I immediately went to the phone to telephone the theater, and a young girl answered. I said, "My daughter has had an accident. Is she badly hurt?" and the girl stammered and almost dropped the phone and said, "J-j-just a minute, it just happened, how did you know?" Then the manager came to the phone, and he said, "Mrs. Hurth, your daughter was hit by a car. She got up and ran to the side of the road, and your husband is with her now. He's going to take her immediately to the doctor. She doesn't seem to be seriously hurt."[3]

Hurth's experience is a common example of telepathy. One person receives a thought or feeling from the mind of another, most often in a time of crisis. According to one study by Dr. Ian Stevenson, a professor of psychiatry at the University of Virginia, nearly 70 percent of telepathic incidents involve close family members. Approximately 28 percent of the time, telepathic communication occurs between friends or acquaintances, and only 2 percent of the time between strangers.

Closer Ties

Some people believe that there are more incidents of telepathy because such people have a stronger mental bond with one another. Others believe that the reason for these statistics lies in the fact that family members and friends are more likely to discuss and consequently verify incidents of telepathy. Bernard Gittelson, in his book *Intangible Evidence*, explains:

> The closer the relationship between the two people involved, the easier it is to verify that telepathy has occurred. They're apt to talk together more (and therefore identify telepathic moments that would otherwise be overlooked), plus they're apt to understand each other more deeply (and therefore be able to distinguish exaggeration, emotionalism, and falsehood from the truth). Telepathy could be happening all the time between strangers as well as friends and relatives—but is it truly telepathy unless it is discovered? Keith Harary [an expert in psychic phenomena] calls this the "Holiday Inn Effect": If a man staying in a hotel had a heart attack and another man staying elsewhere in the hotel had a dream about someone having a heart attack, but checked out of the hotel the

At age five Joicey Hurth's daughter, pictured here, was struck by a car. Although she had no way of knowing what had happened, Hurth had a vision of her daughter involved in an accident.

next day without knowing about the man upstairs, he isn't aware of having had a telepathic experience. And there's no way of knowing how often this type of thing happens.[4]

Such incidents, regardless of whether they occur between family members or strangers, are examples of unintentional telepathy. One person is not trying to send a mental message to another; it just happens. In the case of Joicey Hurth, for example, although her daughter cried out "Mama!" when the accident happened, the girl did not really expect her mother to hear her.

Studying Anecdotal Evidence

Obviously, spontaneous telepathy—particularly the kind associated with a sudden trauma—cannot be tested under laboratory conditions. However, researchers have analyzed reports like Hurth's to see whether there are certain patterns to such stories. In conducting these analyses, researchers use reports that involve witnesses who could corroborate the event. For example, one incident studied by researchers involved a woman who received a feeling from a relative thousands of miles away, in the presence of several witnesses. The woman reported:

> On November 8, 1961, shortly after I had arrived at the school where I teach, I went into the office. Suddenly an extremely severe pain struck my shoulder and chest, so intense that it made me cry out. The principal and other teachers who were in the office were alarmed. However, the intensity of the pain did not last, and I went on with my work.
>
> About an hour after this, my principal came to my room to tell me that I had a long-distance call. My aunt had suffered a heart attack as she and my mother were going downstairs. She had died

Dr. Joseph Banks Rhine and his wife Dr. Louisa Rhine studied parapsychology for many years.

instantly, with only my mother there. As well as we could estimate, it had happened about the time the severe pain had struck me.[5]

The researcher who studied this case was Dr. Louisa Rhine, wife and associate of parapsychologist Joseph Banks (J. B.) Rhine. The two were famous for their laboratory studies of ESP, and they received many unsolicited letters from people reporting their experiences with spontaneous telepathy. Louisa Rhine decided to study these cases in depth. She discovered that approximately 10 percent involved a hallucinated vision, wherein the person

Professor Gilbert Murray had his psychic ability extensively tested by scientists.

sending the message seemed to appear in front of the person receiving it. Approximately 30 percent occurred during a normal waking state, with the message received as a hunch or insight. The remaining 60 percent occurred during a dreaming state.

In many of these dreams, the dreamer "saw" a loved one die or suffer from an accident and shortly after waking discovered that their dream had come true. For example, a grandmother wrote that she had awakened during the night after dreaming that her grandson was smothering in his crib blankets. When the grandmother called her daughter's home to ask that someone check on the baby, her son-in-law reported that he had already done so, and that the baby had indeed been suffocating.

Laboratory Tests

In many cases, people who report an incidence of spontaneous telepathy do not experience repeat episodes. Once the crisis is past, the telepathic ability seems to become dormant. But with intentional telepathy—in which someone purposefully tries to transmit or receive a mental message—some people do seem able to repeat their performance. These apparently gifted psychics have been studied extensively in laboratory tests.

Among the earliest such studies was a series of tests conducted in England in the late nineteenth century. The subject was Professor Gilbert Murray, an Oxford scholar with telepathic ability who came to the attention of the Society for Psychical Research (SPR) during the 1880s.

The SPR was founded in 1882 in Cambridge, England, to investigate paranormal phenomena using scientific methodology. It was the first organization of its kind, and an American branch of the SPR was established in 1884.

The SPR tested Professor Murray by placing him in one room while someone in another room thought of something. Murray would then be asked to describe this person's thoughts. He was correct approximately 30 percent of the time, and even more often when the "sender" was his own daughter.

The SPR concluded that Murray was indeed telepathic, but skeptics of the time period offered an alternate explanation. They believed that Murray was eavesdropping on the comments of the testers in the other room. When this theory was disproved by having the testers remain silent, skeptics suggested that Murray and his daughter simply knew each other so well that one could anticipate what the other might be thinking. Alternatively, Murray and his daughter could have planned their answers in advance.

Skeptics often accused the early SPR testers and their subjects of fraud, so in 1915 an American SPR researcher, Dr. John E. Coover, set out to conduct studies that were as careful and scientifically valid as possible. Whereas most of the first SPR testers had little or no scientific training, Coover was a psychologist well versed in scientific methodology. For his research into telepathy, he used 97 "senders" and 105 "receivers." He placed a receiver in one room and himself and a sender in another, then gave the sender a package of playing cards comprised of aces through tens of all four suits. The sender then looked at each card, selected at random from the pack, and attempted to transmit the image mentally to the receiver. Each sender/receiver pair made approximately one hundred attempts; the entire study involved roughly ten thousand attempts.

Coover concluded that the number of correct guesses in his study—approximately 250—were due to chance or luck. However, subsequent researchers who studied his data argued that there were actually 294 correct guesses, because sometimes the receiver would correctly guess a card that had been selected but set aside and not concentrated upon by the sender. Alfred Douglas, in his book *Extra-Sensory Powers*, explains how this was done:

> After shuffling and cutting the pack, Coover's technique was to throw a die for "odds" or "evens," and depending on which way the die fell the sender would then draw a card and either turn it face up and look at it or else put it aside face down without noting which card it was. Next, Coover tapped the table with his pencil to signal the receiver to write down his impression. The card was then replaced in the pack, which was reshuffled and cut once more. Then the whole process was repeated.[6]

Zener's Cards

Many people who exhibit telepathy in a laboratory setting also exhibit clairvoyance, which is the ability to "see" a picture of some image in the mind without a sender being involved. Therefore it is possible that Coover's test subjects were able to "see" the images on the playing cards that had been set aside. When these discarded images are also taken into account, the number of correct guesses—294—is more than expected by chance. In fact, the odds against such accuracy have been estimated at 160 to 1.

However, there was a flaw in Coover's study and in subsequent studies involving standard playing cards. Because each card has two variables—a number and a suit—it was possible for researchers to influence the results by scoring a guess as correct when only one-half of the answer was right. In other words, if a person guessed the ace of spades and

the card was actually the ace of clubs, the researcher could still score it as correct because it was indeed an ace.

To address this problem, psychologist Karl Zener, who worked with the Rhines, devised a special set of cards for ESP tests. Each card shows one of five symbols—a square (originally a rectangle), a circle, a plus sign, a star, and a set of wavy lines. There are five cards of each symbol in a pack, making twenty-five cards in all. These cards are still used today in a variety of experiments designed to test various forms of ESP, not only in the United States but in Russia, Europe, and other parts of the world as well.

One particularly popular type of study involves the determination of how great distances affect ESP ability. One example of this kind of experiment took place during the *Apollo 14* moon mission. One of the astronauts on this flight, E. D. Mitchell, concentrated on randomly selected ESP cards at prearranged times during his flight, attempting to transmit them mentally to four people on earth. His

Zener cards have simple figures on them instead of the suits and numbers on regular playing cards. This reduces the likelihood of researchers' biases influencing test results.

success rate was no better than chance; in fact, it was somewhat worse. Because of this test and others, researchers have concluded that distance does affect telepathic ability. Some people therefore believe that ESP might be due to some kind of physical process—perhaps the transmission and receipt of energy pulses from the brain—that is dependent on proximity. However, this theory has not been proved. Moreover, distance does not seem to hinder spontaneous telepathy; people have reported receiving messages from loved ones in crisis even when they are continents away.

Hypnosis

Another interesting aspect of telepathy noted by researchers is the fact that a test subject's success rate declines as the test goes on. In other words, the highest number of correct guesses occurs early in the testing process, and as the subject becomes fatigued, the number of correct guesses goes down. Thus, there appears to be a connection between energy level and telepathic ability. But again, the fact that energy might be somehow connected to ESP has not been proved.

Yet another interesting aspect of telepathy involves the use of hypnosis, an altered mental state similar to dreaming. Some experiments have shown that hypnosis heightens telepathic ability. For example, in one series of experiments, a person designated as the telepathic sender was left in a normal waking state while a person designated as the receiver was placed under hypnosis. The two people were in different rooms. The sender was then given a substance like salt or sugar to taste, and the receiver was asked to identify what the sender was tasting. In a similar study, the sender was pinched and the receiver asked what part of the sender's body was experiencing pain. Several of these tests yielded a number of correct answers greater than chance.

Consequently, as with the anecdotes Louisa Rhine studied, it appears that a mind in an altered state is more receptive to telepathic images.

To study this connection further, some parapsychologists have attempted to transmit thoughts, feelings, or images to people who are asleep. For example, in the 1970s researchers at the Maimonides Community Mental Health Center in Brooklyn, New York, had a sender transmit an image to a sleeper while monitoring the sleeper's eyelids for rapid eye movements (REMs), which indicate when someone is dreaming. When awakened in the middle of a dream, people are far more likely to remember dream content, and the Maimonides test subjects were no exception. They were able to describe their dreams in detail, and these descriptions were then analyzed by a panel of judges who did not know which artwork had been used in the test. The judges matched dreams to paintings, and for certain test subjects the rate of success was high. One subject apparently dreamed of the correct image thirteen out of fifteen times.

There are many theories regarding why subjects in a hypnotic or dreaming state do better in ESP tests than those in a normal waking state. One theory is that the subconscious mind is more receptive to psychic connections because it is not distracted by sensory input. To test this theory, researchers have developed another way to isolate the mind from the senses. Called the ESP-ganzfeld experiment (named after the German word *ganzfeld*, which means "entire field" or total environment), it relies on depriving the senses of stimulation.

In the typical ESP-ganzfeld test, the test subject is placed in a special soundproof room that is temperature- and pressure-controlled for maximum comfort. The subject also wears headphones that supply crackling white noise, which prevents the subject from hearing any one specific sound. Special eye covers and lightbulbs are used to make the subject's eyes see a diffused light rather than a specific image. The person placed in this room is the receiver, and various tests are conducted with a sender trying to transmit thoughts, mental images, or feelings to that person.

As with tests using hypnosis and dreaming, the results of ESP-ganzfeld experiments are often better than chance. In fact, the average success rate in over seven hundred ESP-ganzfeld studies conducted at several different laboratories is 34 percent, whereas chance would predict 25 percent. This difference may seem slight, but it is still statistically significant.

The Telepathic Researcher

In these and most other ESP tests, the ability of the receiver is the focus of the experiment. Researchers score the num-

In a ganzfeld experiment, the subject attempts to receive ideas from another person in a separate room. During ganzfeld, the receiver is deprived of sensory stimulation in order to minimize distractions.

ber of correct guesses that person makes. But what of the ability of the sender? There has been much debate over which partner in the telepathic exchange is the most important. There has also been much debate over how a researcher could be sure that the designated sender was really the one sending the message. What if the researcher is really the sender? As Scottish parapsychologist Dr. Robert Morris notes: "There are some people who have argued that all of parapsychology's results are the results of a relatively few gifted and talented experimenters. *They* are actually doing it—manifesting the psi power—and the subject is simply sitting there, coming along for the ride. I don't especially buy that, but it is a possibility."[7]

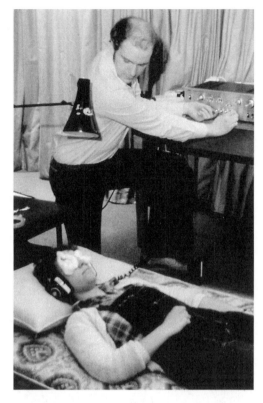

Experimenter Carl Sargent conducts a ganzfeld experiment. One of the great debates of ESP testing is whether or not the experimenter unintentionally affects the results of the experiment.

In *Intangible Evidence*, Gittelson adds another possibility: that researchers might be mentally influencing both senders and receivers. He writes:

> [One] perplexing issue is whether or not the subject in any kind of psi test is safe from the possibility of being unintentionally "psychically" influenced by the people who organize and facilitate the test—an influence that may contaminate the result, even though, ironically, it may in itself be a sign of psi in operation. Known as the "experimenter effect," it's one of the more fascinating paradoxes involved in the struggle to analyze psi ability. . . . A major concern relating to the experimenter effect is that a subject's performance may be considerably altered by the mere expectations of the person conducting

the experiment. It has long been observed that some researchers consistently get better results than others, with identical experiment protocols.[8]

Gittelson reports that there are many examples of researchers who appear to be mentally affecting the outcome of their experiments, not only in paranormal research but in other types of scientific research as well, as he explains:

> The experimenter effect can take place in any of the life sciences. In a laboratory test that has become a classic illustration of this curious phenomenon, rats chosen for their similar abilities in maze-running were randomly grouped into two separate cages, one marked "clever" and the other marked "stupid." Each rat was then tested in a series of maze-runs by several different research assistants. The rats taken from the cage marked "clever" invariably produced the better scores, even though the population of each cage was secretly and randomly changed after each run. Could the subjects in a telepathy experiment—or any other experiment for psi ability—be susceptible to a similar performance catalyst? Perhaps wishing *does* make it so.[9]

Apparently, the researchers' expectations that one rat would do well and another do badly influenced their behavior. This might be the case with ESP research as well. Once a particular receiver is identified as "gifted," the expectations regarding that person's success rate could influence how many correct guesses are made overall. There is also evidence that a researcher's thoughts can intrude on a telepathic person's dreams. As an example, Gittelson quotes from the writings of psychiatrist Montague Ullman, who reports on one of the most famous cases of dream intrusion between a therapist and a patient:

In his dream, the patient offered a chromium soap dish to a man who blushed when the patient said, "Well, you're building a house." The patient could not report any associates to the soap dish. However, the therapist remembered that a year and a half earlier, a chromium soap dish had, by mistake, been shipped to the new house into which he had just moved. In a belligerent spirit, responding to the mounting building costs, he never bothered to return it; but a week before the patient's dream, several architects had come over to inspect the house; and one had spied the soap dish lying unused in the cellar, and had embarrassed the therapist by calling attention to it.[10]

Telepathy and Clairvoyance

Such stories suggest that a telepathic person might be influenced by anyone present during a test, not just the designated sender. But this is not the only kind of identity confusion related to ESP testing. It is also sometimes difficult for researchers to determine whether the ESP skill being displayed is telepathy or clairvoyance. A clairvoyant person can see mental pictures of distant places or objects, and in tests for telepathy involving card symbols, it is possible that the receiver is getting the mental images not from the sender but from the cards themselves. In fact, this might be true in experiments involving other types of visual images as well. As John Taylor notes in his book *Science and the Supernatural*, "It is difficult to distinguish a clairvoyant perception of a distant location from the telepathic proving of someone else's thoughts, and especially memories, of that place."[11]

Consequently many researchers no longer test for either telepathy or clairvoyance. Instead they test for both abilities together. This combination is known as general

ESP, or GESP. Meanwhile other researchers have attempted to develop experiments that will test for telepathy without the possibility of clairvoyance being involved and vice versa. But regardless of what is being tested or how, it is still difficult to determine all of the human forces at work during the testing process. It is also difficult to prove without doubt that anything other than luck is involved in successful studies.

Chapter 2

Clairvoyance

One day a man lost his watch while working in a friend's vast fields. A few nights later, the friend dreamed that he saw the watch lying in a certain way in a certain place. The next morning he felt sure that this was where the watch really was, and he excitedly told his friend where to find it. When the two men went together to that location, the watch was exactly as it had appeared in the dream.

In *Borderlands*, Mike Dash points out that the image of the watch was apparently not transmitted by telepathy because "it is unlikely that the watch's owner or anyone else had seen it lying in the position in which it was found."[12] Therefore the watch dream was an episode of clairvoyance, wherein an accurate image of an object or event appears in a person's mind. Unlike telepathy, clairvoyance is not mind-to-mind communication; the image is not transmitted by a human sender.

Telepathy or Clairvoyance?

It is often difficult for researchers to determine whether telepathy or clairvoyance is being used during a particular ESP episode. This is true not only in regard to laboratory tests but also in incidents of spontaneous ESP. Sometimes in examining reports of ESP, experts disagree on whether a human sender was indeed involved.

For example, one day a pilot flying a single-engine plane suddenly decided to go seventy miles out of her way, where she spotted a crashed car beside the road below. She landed her plane and rescued the unconscious passenger, only to discover it was her mother. As Bernard Gittelson notes in *Intangible Evidence*, some experts would call this a case of telepathy triggered by a crisis. But the woman in the car was unconscious and therefore—or so Gittelson suggests—could not have transmitted a mental image of her crisis to her daughter. Moreover, even if the woman was able to transmit such a message while unconscious, she certainly could not have known how to direct her daughter to her location, particularly since all physical references would have been seen from the air. Consequently, Gittelson continues,

This retriever is said to have revealed his death to his owner, Rider Haggard, in a dream so detailed Haggard was later able to find the body of the dead dog.

at first glance, the young pilot's story seems to illustrate telepathy: Someone very important to her has an urgent need for help, and she is instantly aware of this need, though she is physically distant from that person and preoccupied with her own activity. What makes the story distinctive, however, is not her sensitivity in itself, which, after all, was not focused on a particular person and did not take the form of a coherent thought, feeling, or emotion. The remarkable part is her ability to go directly to the scene of the need, despite the fact that she had no rational way of determining where it was.[13]

Gittelson cites another case of clairvoyance that others might call telepathy. He tells of a Canadian news reporter who in 1963 was in the middle of describing Queen Elizabeth's appearance in a royal procession on the air when suddenly he began describing President John F. Kennedy's motorcade instead. The image of this motorcade came to him clearly, along with a feeling of nausea, but he could not explain why he saw the image or why he began talking about it. Shortly thereafter he discovered that his description of the scene was accurate and coincided with the president's assassination during the motorcade. Was this image transmitted via clairvoyance, or did the minds of the people witnessing the scene transmit it telepathically?

Isolating Clairvoyance

Disagreements over whether clairvoyance or telepathy was involved in a particular ESP incident have long plagued psychic researchers. In fact, when ESP was first studied by the SPR in the late nineteenth and early twentieth centuries, researchers did not believe that clairvoyance existed, only telepathy. When someone in a laboratory test exhibited the ability to know what was on a playing card before pulling it from the deck, for example, researchers thought it was because the person conducting the test knew the order of the cards beforehand and was unintentionally transmitting this information to the test subject via telepathy.

Consequently in the 1930s parapsychologists J. B. and Louisa Rhine, then at Duke University, set out to prove that clairvoyance truly existed. It was J. B. Rhine who encouraged Zener to create his special cards for ESP testing; the Rhines used these cards extensively to test for

Extra-Sensory Perception

J. B. RHINE, Ph. D.
Associate Professor of Psychology
Duke University

With a Foreword by
Professor WILLIAM McDOUGALL, F.R.S., D.Sc., M.B.

And an Introduction by
WALTER FRANKLIN PRINCE, Ph.D.
Research Officer, B.S.P.R.

MARCH, 1934
BOSTON SOCIETY FOR PSYCHIC RESEARCH
719 Boylston Street, Boston, Mass.

The title page of J. B. Rhine's first published account of ESP, based on his experiments.

clairvoyance. They made sure that testers did not know the order of the cards not only before but during the test, and they devised new methods for eliminating the possibility that telepathy was involved. H. J. Irwin, in his book *An Introduction to Parapsychology*, explains:

Several different experimental techniques were devised by the Rhines. Two are methods for testing clairvoyance. In the "down-through" (DT) technique the subject has to guess the order of symbols in a shuffled downward-facing deck, starting from the top and working down. After the 25 guesses are recorded, each card is turned over and checked against the subject's corresponding call. In an alternative technique the experimenter takes one card at a time from the shuffled pack, places it face down, records the subject's call, and then repeats the process until all 25 cards have been used. The calls and targets finally are checked for correspondence.[14]

The Rhines took many other steps to ensure that their research was valid. For example, they made sure that test subjects could not see or hear the experimenter, because they realized that by noticing the experimenter's facial expression or tone of voice, a test subject might know whether a guess was correct. With this knowledge, a clever test subject would realize that if a deck contained only five circle symbols, for example, and one of them had already been selected, then only four remained; this awareness might influence subsequent guesses. The Rhines also realized that the first sets of Zener's cards were not uniform on the back side. Some had one pattern while others had a slightly different one, which meant that in repeat tests a subject might know which card was which just from looking at the back. They therefore had the cards changed so that when face down all of them looked alike.

Impressive Results

Whereas previous ESP tests had few safeguards against cheating, the Rhines' experiments seemed to be well designed against fraud. Nonetheless, when some of their results suggested that clairvoyance was a real phenomenon, skeptics accused the Rhines' test subjects of cheating. Skeptics were particularly critical of one of the Rhines' most successful clairvoyants, a student at Duke University named Hubert Pearce.

During tests of his clairvoyance, Pearce was placed in one room while in another room a researcher named J. G. Pratt turned over cards in a pack and recorded their order, without trying to transmit them telepathically to Pearce. These two rooms were in completely different buildings, a hundred yards apart. But despite this distance, after it was revealed that Pearce had gotten 558 out of 1850 guesses right—when only 370 would have been expected by chance—skeptics accused Pearce of peeking at the cards. John Taylor explains:

> These results [with Pearce] were later criticized by [skeptic] C. E. M. Hansel, who pointed out that Pearce could have gone to Pratt's building and looked through the fanlight of Pratt's door to see the cards Pratt was handling or the score sheet. That Pearce could have attempted this is true, but further

Researcher J. G. Pratt uses cards in an experiment testing Hubert Pearce's abilities. The two are in separate rooms 250 feet apart.

analysis claimed to have shown that neither cards nor score sheet would have been visible from that position. In particular, American parapsychologist Ian Stevenson claims that Hansel based his conclusion on an inaccurate diagram of Pratt's office.[15]

The Rhines found several other subjects whose guesses on similar tests were also much better than chance. Other researchers found gifted clairvoyants as well—not only human ones but animals. For example, in the late 1950s parapsychologist Remi Cadoret of Duke University conducted a series of tests on a dog named Chris. Before coming to Cadoret's attention, Chris had demonstrated the ability to tap his owner the correct number of times when told that number. At Cadoret's behest, the dog was trained to paw the floor a certain number of times when he was shown a particular symbol from Zener's cards—once for the circle, twice for the plus sign, and so on. Individual cards were then placed in black envelopes that were mixed up so that no one knew which Zener card was in which envelope. Upon being shown an envelope, Chris would be directed to paw out a number of his choosing.

A long series of such tests revealed some impressive results: Chris was right most of the time. Alfred Douglas, in *Extra-Sensory Powers*, explains:

> No one was aware of the order of the cards before each test was completed and checked, so simple telepathy between dog and human could not be the answer. The only alternatives were that the dog was either a talented clairvoyant, or else he was reacting to slight sensory cues from one of the humans present who was unconsciously exercising ESP. One series of tests gave results of the order of a thousand million to one against chance expectation.[16]

Remote Viewing

While researchers like Remi Cadoret were studying animal clairvoyants, the U.S. Army was investigating a more practical use for ESP. In the 1970s the government began a top-secret project to discover whether human clairvoyants might be used to "see" distant military targets and spy on enemies. Originally code-named GRILLFLAME but eventually called STARGATE, this project began at the Stanford Research Institute (SRI) in California and lasted at least until 1995, when the government acknowledged the project and claimed to have ended it. Much about the project remains secret, although two of its participants, David Morehouse and Joseph McMoneagle, have written about it—Morehouse in his book *Psychic Warrior: Inside the CIA's Stargate Program* (1996) and McMoneagle in *Mind Trek: Exploring Consciousness, Time, and Space Through Remote Viewing* (1993; revised in 1997). McMoneagle, who was a part of the project from beginning to end under the designation Viewer #001, reports that "99% of the data, files, missions, and methods utilized by the project are still classified and sealed within boxes."[17]

Nonetheless, the basics of the SRI remote-viewing tests are known. In the earliest experiments, one or more people, called outbounders, were sent to a particular location, or target, unknown to the test subject or the interviewer in the room with him during the test. Once the outbounders were in place, the subject would verbally describe and then sketch any impressions or images he might be receiving. In later tests, instead of using outbounders, photographs were taken of several targets prior to the test and sealed in an envelope. One envelope was then selected at random and the test subject asked to describe and sketch its contents. In some of the last series of tests, no photographs were taken nor outbounders used. Instead the targets were identified only through geographical coordinates picked at random; the actual locations were not visited until after the remote viewer had finished describing them. This ruled out the possibility that telepathy rather than clairvoyance was involved.

The success rates of many of these tests have not been reported. However, McMoneagle claims that in his first series of tests, he provided enough information on five out of six targets for a stranger to be able to recognize the locations from his descriptions and drawings. But he also admits that his success rate was uneven. In his next series of tests, he failed to identify twenty-four out of twenty-four targets.

McMoneagle does not see these as failures, though. He believes that his poor results were due to his inability to understand the visual cues he was receiving. He explains:

> In remote viewing there are failures for the scientists, there are failures for the judges [who objectively determine whether the drawings are accurate], there are failures for the observers—but *there are no failures for the remote viewer. . . .* What the remote

viewer is actually trying to do is to translate symbols and images from the mind into knowledgeable statements about a remote target. For example, if I am working a remote target and see a sideways < in my mind, I might translate it to mean the bow of a ship. Upon seeing the actual target, I will find out that it wasn't the bow of a ship; it was a church. The scientist sees a failure, the judges see failure, any observer sees failure, but what I *see* is that a sideways < is part of my mental picture of a church. I have learned something, so I have not failed. Right or wrong, I am learning and squeezing 100% from the experience.[18]

In other words, once the remote viewer learns that his mind equates a church with the < symbol, he will be able to identify a church in the future. The remote-viewing mental images are like a code.

Moreover, in at least one instance, McMoneagle discovered that an apparent failure was actually a success. He viewed the correct images at a target location—but in the wrong time period, as he recounts:

> In early 1984 I worked a string of six targets in the lab at SRI-International, two of which were judged as dismal failures. They were rife with exquisite detail, but the details had nothing in common with the actual targeted sites. One was a lumber yard attached to a small hardware store, and the other was an old BART

Joseph McMoneagle's vision of a parking lot is an example of remote viewing that not only transcends space but also time.

train station and platform. I described the first as a multi-story high-tech building with off-set balconies and hanging gardens, the second as a parking lot. . . . Almost a year later, after flying out to the West Coast to participate in a series of new experiments, I was driving to my hotel from the airport the evening I arrived and was somewhat surprised to find the first of my two misses had been bulldozed away and replaced with a new building of concrete and glass. The balconies of the building were offset and had lots of green plants hanging from their ledges. I noticed this simply because it looked exactly like the image that I had in my mind the previous year. After checking into my hotel, I drove my rental car to the second target site and was even more pleased when greeted by a brand-new parking lot.[19]

Apparently, McMoneagle's ability to transcend space was accompanied by the ability to transcend time. And interestingly, when he went back to study the files on his initial description of these sites, he found that whereas during most of the tests he had been told the time and date that the target had been acquired, in this case the researchers had omitted that information. Therefore he believes his mind felt free to go to any time it found interesting.

McMoneagle continues to practice remote viewing today as a research associate at the Laboratories for Fundamental Research, a psychic research facility in Palo Alto, California. Even though the military has apparently discontinued its investigations of remote viewing, he believes that it has many practical uses, particularly in providing information on terrorist strongholds. However, he notes that the accuracy of remote viewing varies widely, and he explains that remote viewers generally cannot provide information about the location of a person or object. In other words, they cannot be used to find a lost child or possession.

Psychic Detectives

But another type of clairvoyant can be used for such things. Typically referred to as a psychic detective, this person can receive images or impressions about the victims of crimes or tragedies. Approximately 37 percent of America's urban police departments admit to having used psychic detectives at least once, with varying degrees of success. These psychics use a variety of methods to receive information about a crime. Sometimes they obtain an image of an event without having foreknowledge of that event. Other times they must visit the scene of the event

"Psychic Cop" Keith Charles. Known as psychic detectives, individuals like Charles use various methods to provide more information about crimes.

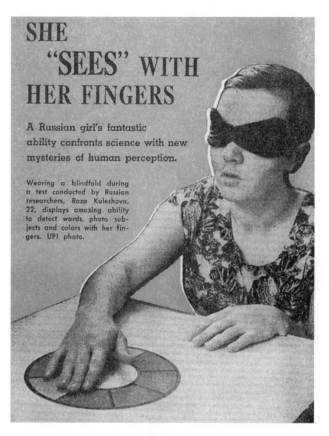

SHE "SEES" WITH HER FINGERS

A Russian girl's fantastic ability confronts science with new mysteries of human perception.

Wearing a blindfold during a test conducted by Russian researchers, Roza Kuleshova, 22, displays amazing ability to detect words, photo subjects and colors with her fingers. UPI photo.

Russian psychic Roza Kuleshova can "see" color and words simply by touching colored objects and printed text. ESP that occurs by touching is called psychometry.

or handle an object associated with it before they can receive an image.

In regard to the handling of objects, a link between touch and clairvoyance has been shown in several laboratory studies. For example, in the 1960s researchers in what was then the Soviet Union conducted a series of tests on a girl named Roza Kuleshova, who demonstrated the ability to "read" text and "see" colors while blindfolded simply by running her fingers over printed words or touching colored objects. This ability to discover facts via ESP by touching or being near an object is called psychometry. In his book *The Directory of Psychics*, Hans Holzer, an expert on psychic phenomena, offers the most prevalent theory regarding how psychometry works:

Psychometry is based on the theory that emotional events create a thin film that permanently coats all persons or objects in the immediate vicinity. A psychometrist coming in contact with the persons or objects will be able to read the coating and thus will be able to reconstruct the emotional event. Most psychometry concerns the past, some of it bears on the present, and occasionally it will pertain to the future. Some psychometrists need to touch an object that has been on the person to be investigated, while others get stimuli simply by being in the immediate vicinity of the person. Professional mediums [i.e., psychics] have been able to locate lost persons by touching objects belonging to the persons and reconstructing their immediate pasts.[20]

Many prominent psychics throughout history have used touch and location to tell them about past crimes. For example, Peter Hurkos solved a notorious crime in 1958 after holding a photograph of a missing cabdriver and sitting in his cab. He was able to give police a complete description of the man's killer, along with the killer's hometown, nickname, and information about another crime committed by the same person.

In the 1980s, psychic investigator Lawrence LeShan conducted tests on a noted psychic, Eileen Garrett, who appeared to be skilled in psychometry. Gittelson reports on this study in *Intangible Evidence:*

First [LeShan] showed [Garrett] three identical boxes and told her what was inside each of them: One contained a lock of hair from his daughter Wendy, one contained a tuft from the tail of his neighbor's dog, and one contained a rosebud. Then he took the boxes behind a screen setup which allowed Garrett to hold the boxes through sleeves without actually seeing them. In an order determined by random-number tables, he slid each box beneath her fingers. She was always able to identify correctly the contents of the box and to deliver commentary that astonished LeShan.[21]

As an example of this commentary, after touching the box with Wendy's hair in it, Garrett said that the girl would prefer to be called Hilary. LeShan confirmed that his daughter had once asked to have her name changed to

Hilary because she liked it; this fact had never been related to anyone outside of the immediate family. Garrett also said that the girl was going to be joining something like the Peace Corps during the summer. An astonished LeShan confirmed that Wendy was going to be at camp during the summer, and he and his wife had been referring to it as "a junior Peace Corps."[22]

Garrett's knowledge appears to have been triggered by touch, but there are other psychics who receive information without any physical prompt. This is particularly true for people who have clairaudience or clairsentience. Whereas clairvoyance is the receipt of visual images via ESP, clairaudience is the receipt of sounds via ESP and clairsentience

Eileen Garrett's ESP abilities have been tested by allowing her to touch objects hidden inside boxes.

of thoughts and ideas. The term *clairsentience* is also sometimes used to refer to people who receive smells or tastes via ESP.

Garrett's receipt of information about Wendy is an example of the former definition of clairsentience. An example of the latter would be a person "smelling" smoke from a fire that occurred several years in the past. An example of clairaudience would be an instance where someone "hears" a voice warning them of a real but hidden danger when no one else is present.

Some people who appear to have clairaudience claim that the voices they hear come from the spirits of people long dead. This is the case with Sylvia Brown, one of the most popular clairvoyants in America. Brown has often been asked to find missing persons or help police solve crimes. She says that her information comes either through clairvoyance or through information she receives from a spirit guide named Francine.

Brown does not need to touch anything to trigger her clairvoyance or clairsentience, nor does she need to visit a crime scene. When asked about a crime, she simply "sees" or "knows" information about it. Moreover, in many cases the information she receives relates not just to the present but to the future as well. As an example, in 1987 police in Los Altos, California, asked Brown about a serial rapist. She was immediately able to describe him and report that his last name began with an "S." She also said that his job required him to work under the street. Then she went one step further: she predicted where he would strike next, saying, "It's going to happen next in Redwood City. . . . You better start doubling up [your police patrols] in Redwood City, because that's where you're going to catch him. He's thinking about Redwood City. He wants to rape someone there, but instead you'll get him."[23]

The police did indeed catch the rapist in Redwood City. His name was George Anthony Sanchez, and his job was repairing sewers.

The ability to predict the future, known as precognition, appears to be common among clairvoyants; just as telepathy and clairvoyance are often linked, so too are clairvoyance and precognition. These overlapping skills add to the difficulties that researchers have in explaining ESP.

Chapter 3

Precognition

Research into psychic ability has focused primarily on testing telepathic or clairvoyant messages sent in real time. But according to Dr. Richard S. Broughton, a leading investigator into psychic phenomena, more than half of all psychic experiences impart information about events that have not yet occurred. In *Parapsychology: The Controversial Science*, he gives an example of such an experience:

> [A woman] had a vivid dream in which her husband was out hunting and had been accidentally shot and killed by his hunting partner. It had been an unusually vivid dream—unlike her normal dreams—and she had awakened from it in a cold sweat. Her husband did go hunting occasionally and she debated whether or not she should tell him about the dream. Since he had no immediate plans to go hunting and he had already announced that his schedule would not permit him to do so that season, the woman decided not to mention the dream. About two weeks later her husband was unexpectedly invited to go hunting, and equally unexpectedly he found the time to do so. Again the woman debated whether or not to tell him about the dream, but this time she feared that perhaps the act of telling him might somehow bring the event to pass, and she knew in any case that her hus-

band would ridicule her concern over "just a dream."
. . . The next morning her husband did go hunting,
and in a freak accident almost exactly like the one
the woman had seen in her dream, his partner acci-
dentally shot and killed him.[24]

The Theory of Relativity

This incident is an example of precognition, which provides a specific image of or clear information about an
event that will occur in the future. Scientists disagree
regarding whether or not people can actually "see" an event
that has not yet occurred. Many, however, do believe that
the future exists even as the present is taking place.

The basis for this belief lies in scientist Albert Einstein's
special theory of relativity. In 1905 Einstein argued, among
other things, that space and time are closely related.

Albert Einstein's theories about relativity, the relationship between space and time, have been used by researchers studying ESP to explain how the future can exist even as the present is taking place.

According to Einstein's theory, the speed at which one
travels affects how rapidly or
slowly one ages, and the clos-
er one gets to the speed of
light, the more slowly he or
she ages. Someone traveling
as fast as the speed of light,
were that possible, would not
age at all. Someone traveling
even faster than the speed of
light would go backward in
time. Theodore Schick Jr.
and Lewis Vaughn, in their
book *How to Think About
Weird Things*, explain how
this concept defines the relationship between past, present, and future:

Einstein's discovery that space and time are related is often expressed by saying that time is a fourth dimension. What this means is that time is as much a direction of travel as are the directions up-down, right-left, and forward-backward. Objects travel through both space and time. . . . From a fourth-dimensional point of view, then, all of the moments of your life exist simultaneously. . . . [Therefore] it is both logically and physically possible for the future to exist now.[25]

According to Schick and Vaughn, if the present and the future exist simultaneously, then time is like a series of frames in a motion picture. The entire movie already exists and cannot be changed, but the way we interpret it depends on how it is projected. Schick and Vaughn explain:

Four-dimensional objects can create the illusion of change by being projected onto the screen of consciousness one slice at a time. Ordinarily, each slice is projected in sequence. In the case of precognition, however, slices are taken out of order. The mind skips ahead, so to speak. As a result, we are aware of something "before" it happens.

But Schick and Vaughn also point out that this theory has never been proved, saying: "Even if precognition doesn't violate any physical laws, it may not occur. From the fact that something can happen, it doesn't follow that it does happen."[26]

Anecdotal Evidence

Nonetheless, there are many anecdotes regarding people's ability to predict a future event. One of the most famous cases concerns President Abraham Lincoln. In 1865 he had a dream that was so unsettling he shared it with friends. He told them: "Before me was a catafalque [a support for a coffin] on which rested a corpse wrapped in funeral vestments. Around it were stationed soldiers who were gazing mournfully upon the corpse."[27] In his dream, Lincoln asked someone the identity of the corpse and was told it was the president of the United States. One week after having this dream, Lincoln was assassinated.

Another famous case of precognition was even better documented. In 1898 an author named Morgan Robertson wrote a novel about an ocean liner named *Titan* that strikes an iceberg in the northern Atlantic Ocean one April. In April 1912, the ocean liner *Titanic* struck an iceberg in the northern Atlantic Ocean. In addition, many of the details in Robertson's story were similar to the actual events related to the *Titanic*'s sinking.

One of the most famous cases of precognition involves Abraham Lincoln, who told friends about a dream in which he died, just a week before being assassinated.

According to Bernard Gittelson, although instances of precognition that involve major catastrophes like the sinking of the *Titanic* receive the most attention in the press, "the major proportion of anecdotal material consists of precognitions relating to one's personal fate."[28] For example, Sir Winston Churchill had precognitive experiences, but they did not relate to the events of World War II, which took place during his time as British prime minister. Instead they generally had to do with his personal safety and well-being. Gittelson cites one incident reported by Churchill's wife:

> In Lady Churchill's autobiography, she tells about a time during World War II when her husband . . . was

preparing to return to Downing Street after an inspection tour of London. He was just about to get in on the street side of his staff car, as he always did, when "for no apparent reason he stopped, turned, opened the door on the other side of the car himself, got in, and sat there instead"—something she had never seen him do. On the way back, a bomb fell near the car and would have hurled it over, if Churchill had sat in his usual place. "Only Winston's extra weight," Lady Churchill insists, "had prevented disaster." When she asked her husband about the incident, he could say only that "something" had made him stop, in a way that told him to sit on the other side. Later, Churchill told a miners' group, "I sometimes have a feeling—in fact, I have had it very strongly—a feeling of interference. I want to stress it. I have a feeling sometimes that some guiding hand has interfered."[29]

British prime minister Winston Churchill experienced premonitions about his safety during World War II. One of these premonitions saved him and his wife from being hurt in a bomb explosion.

Premonitions

Churchill's vague feelings are representative of the mildest form of precognitive experience, the premonition. Unlike more vivid precognitive experiences, such as Lincoln's dream, they do not involve specific images rich with detail. Instead they are mere hunches. Gittelson reports that premonitions are the most common type of precognitive experience.

According to Hans Holzer in *The Directory of Psychics*, there are many degrees of precognition. In the case of premonitions, some are as vague as Churchill's, while others have enough details for the person experiencing the event—also called the experient—to know not only that something bad is going to happen but exactly what that something will be. As an example of a premonition with such detail, Holzer cites the case of Lorna Middleton, a piano teacher in London, England, who on several different days in 1968 experienced a strong feeling that Senator Robert Kennedy would be assassinated. She decided to report her premonitions to researchers who had established a registry for precognitive experiences, and when Kennedy was indeed killed her premonitions were verified as accurate.

Middleton's predictions were among 469 individual premonitions registered with the researchers; eighteen proved accurate, with Middleton and one other individual providing twelve of those correct premonitions. There have been several other premonition registries established over the years, to varying degrees of success. One such registry, the Central Premonitions Registry in New York, also received a correct prediction of Robert Kennedy's assassination prior to the event. It came from psychic Alan Vaughan, who had a dream about Kennedy being shot in a kitchen hallway, which was where the assassination ultimately took place.

Although there were only two registered predictions of this major event, some researchers believe that there might have been many more. As Holzer points out, few people are eager to register their premonitions:

> Unfortunately, the majority of people who have premonitory experiences never bother to register them with anyone because most concern disaster or

negative aspects of life. Receivers are afraid to bring bad news and frequently prefer to dismiss their impressions or actively suppress them. As a result, much valuable psychic material is undoubtedly lost to science, and where there might have been warnings, and possibly prevention of a disaster, there are only the faits accompli [i.e., the end result].[30]

Indeed, studies have shown that 85 percent of all precognitive information relates to death or disaster. Moreover, far more women experience precognition than men, and of these women the majority are in their mid-forties. Many of these women fear that if they were to report their predictions, they would not be believed.

Another reason that people are hesitant to report premonitions is because of the vague nature of their experiences. People who have premonitions often wonder whether they are simply manifestations of their own fears or anxiety. However, even when filled with doubt, many people do seem to alter their behavior in accordance with their premonitions. In *Borderlands*, Mike Dash reports on an interesting study that apparently proves this:

> In the early 1960s the American parapsychologist William Cox collected detailed statistics which compared the number of passengers travelling on trains that had been involved in a collision or accident with the number travelling on the same train on each of the preceding seven days, and on three sample days in the previous month. His results showed that, in each case, there were fewer passengers on the damaged or derailed trains than normal; analysing his figures, he concluded that the odds against this effect happening by chance were more than 100 to 1. This suggests, of course, that some prospective passengers had experienced premonitions and chosen not to travel on the fateful day.[31]

Vivid Precognitive Events

People are even more likely to heed their predictions when they come in the form of vivid precognitive experiences. One example of this is the case of John Godley, who later became known as Lord Kilbracken. In 1946, while an undergraduate at Oxford University in England, Godley dreamed that he was looking at a written account of some horse races that listed the winners. The next day he learned that two of the horses he had "read" about in his dream were indeed running a race that day. He mentioned this to some friends, who encouraged him to bet on the horses. They won.

Godley had several more racing dreams over the course of the year. He continued to see the names of winners, and often saw statistics regarding their odds of winning as well. Each time he told friends about his dreams and placed bets in accordance with those dreams. In all but two instances he—and the friends who had confidence in his abilities—won money on those bets.

Parapsychologist William Cox has studied train wrecks and found that trains involved in such accidents often are holding fewer passengers than normal. He attributes this discovery to people experiencing premonitions of such mishaps.

In Godley's case, he received just enough information to act on his dreams. This does not always happen. Holzer reports that just as with premonitions, vivid precognitive experiences like Godley's can either provide a lot of information about a future event or very little. Regarding the latter, Holzer says that a person might foresee a future event "without 'getting' any specifics about time and place, mainly receiving only the basic message." Moreover, when such a message is received while the experient is dreaming, it might be told via symbolic images rather than actual ones. Holzer gives an example of a precognitive dream in which symbolism is used to convey a message:

> For instance, in a precognitive dream, your brother has bought a new car, which he wants to show you. The following day he phones to tell you that he is going to visit you in the near future. When he arrives, it turns out that he has just remarried and wants you to meet his bride. In the dream the car was a symbol for the new wife.[32]

Holzer adds that when transmitted to someone in a waking state rather than to a dreamer, the same precognitive message would not be as likely to use symbolism. However, it still might not provide the experient with enough details to offer a clear prediction of the future, particularly in regard to the time and place the event is going to occur.

Precognitive experiences that do feature information relating to time and place might still not provide enough details for the experient to act on them. According to Holzer, information in such experiences "may be only partial, such as a numeral 'flashed' above the face of the person in the vision, or a key word spoken by an inner voice that relates to the circumstances of the future event."

Alternatively, the information might be clear and precise. Holzer reports that in general, the more extreme the incident the greater the likelihood that clear information will be provided, as he explains:

> If it [i.e., the future event] is merely routine, although it may be of some emotional significance to the receiver, the message is less likely to contain dramatic descriptive material than if it concerned a catastrophe, a dire event, or a situation of importance to more than one person. For instance, clairvoyants who are able to predict plane crashes (a specialty among some) do so in great detail. The same appears to be true for those who predict fires and earthquakes.[33]

Unreliable Information

Predictions by professional psychics are often published in magazines and newspapers. According to records kept by the SPR, these predictions are usually wrong. For example, in 1997 professional psychics publicly announced dozens of false predictions, including one stating that the movie *Gone with the Wind* would be made into a musical. That same year professional psychics also failed to predict the death of Princess Diana. That such a significant tragedy was not predicted is not unusual, as Dash reports:

> The evidence for precognition of impending disaster is essentially negative; in other words, there are no accurate predictions of events that one might reasonably expect to have been predicted. Of all the catastrophes of the twentieth-century, the greatest were the two world wars. Yet not only do there appear to have been no good predictions of the coming disasters, each destined to affect many millions

of families around the world, but throughout the tense months leading to the outbreak of the Second World War, when even lay people were becoming increasingly certain that a conflict was inevitable, the . . . [psychics] continued to insist that there would be no war. The same failure occurred in 1982, when Argentina invaded the Falkland Islands. On the other hand, the leader of a variety of cults and religious movements have given several dozen, very specific dates for the end of the world, ranging from 1843 to 2012—predictions that seemed real enough to persuade thousands of their followers to devote themselves to preparing for the doomsday. To date, it goes without saying, not one of those predictions has been fulfilled.[34]

American invaders approach the beach at the Battle of Normandy during World War II. Surprisingly, events such as wars that can affect millions of lives around the world generally are not predicted by psychics.

Several studies have shown that vivid precognitive experiences are so unreliable that they cannot be trusted. For example, in a study of twelve hundred reports of vivid precognition that occurred between 1967 and 1973, fewer than a dozen provided any degree of accuracy. Moreover, there was no significant increase in reports of precognition prior to a major disaster during those years.

Altering the Future

Still, there continue to be cases like that of John Godley, where people not only apparently predict the future but use their predictions in order to make decisions. In some cases, it appears that such people are actually able to alter the future. For example, in the 1930s parapsychologist Louisa Rhine studied 191 precognitive experiences involving subsequent attempts to change the future. In 60, or 31 percent, of these cases, the person who experienced the precognition was unable to stop a predicted event from happening, often because of incomplete information. But in 131, or 69 percent, the person was successful in stopping the event, typically because the precognitive dream was rich in detail.

One example of someone who was unable to stop a predicted event was a woman who dreamed of a fiery plane crash at the shore of a nearby lake. Although she told friends about her dream, she did not contact any authorities because she did not know the airline or the time the event would occur. A few days later she saw a particular plane flying overhead and recognized it as the plane in her dream. She told her husband to alert the fire department so their personnel would be on hand to douse the flames, but by then it was too late. The crash had already occurred.

In another case, a streetcar conductor who dreamed of a fatal crash involving his streetcar and a truck was able to stop the event. In his dream, he clearly saw the precise route of the streetcar as well as a vivid picture of the truck and its occupants. While at work the next day, he recognized a series of events as being part of his dream, and he realized that the crash was about to occur. He suddenly stopped his streetcar—barely in time to miss hitting a truck that matched the one he had envisioned.

Laboratory Tests

Fascinated by such stories, some researchers have tried to create tests that will prove precognition is a real ability. As with telepathy and clairvoyance, they at first used cards and photographs to see whether people could predict what card or photo would be chosen next. However, Helmut Schmidt, a physicist working for a psychic research center called the Mind Science Foundation in San Antonio, Texas, recognized that there were problems with using such tests in association with precognition. In particular, he felt that it was difficult to ensure that precognition was being used instead of telepathy or psychokinesis, a mental ability whereby the mind is able to influence matter. Since human beings were always responsible for providing the card deck and selecting which cards were drawn, Schmidt argued that no one could guarantee that the selection of a particular card was not being influenced by mind-to-mind communication between subject and tester. He also argued that a test subject with psychokinetic ability might be able to influence the shuffle of the cards.

Therefore Schmidt invented a machine that produced a random event that no researcher could influence. It flashed lights in a pattern determined by the decay of a radioactive isotope called strontium 90; the rate of decay was completely unpredictable, which meant that the pattern of the lights was also completely unpredictable. Researchers have been using the Schmidt machine for several years, and according to Gittelson: "So far, experiments with the Schmidt machine have helped both to verify the existence of precognition and to facilitate the examination of a large

number of subjects under the same tightly controlled con-ditions."[35] However, as with tests for telepathy and clair-voyance, skeptics argue that correct guesses regarding the patterns of the lights are due to luck.

Physicist Helmut Schmidt devised a machine to produce random events so that no one can unintentionally affect experiments in precognition.

Explaining the Results

The idea that the future can be predicted, let alone changed, is impossible to believe for some people. Yet it is difficult to account for cases in which people do predict events, particularly when they act on those predictions and seem to alter the future. As Holzer points out:

> Persons who hold up the failures of predictions to materialize as proof of their fallacy are reminded that *any* prediction's coming true is a surprise if we use the old-fashioned laws of probability as a mea-suring stick. By those standards, if 98 percent of all the predictions that are made were tabulated and

found to be incorrect and 2 percent were found to be correct, that would be 2 percent too many. The proven reality of even 2 percent of all predictions would pose a challenge to the scientific community that could not be ignored. If predictions can come true at all, something is lacking in the law of cause and effect, something requiring further study and, ultimately, a reevaluation of that law.[36]

Skeptics counter that since relatively few people register their predictions with ESP researchers, a 2 percent accuracy rate is very small and could easily be due to luck or coincidence. Moreover, skeptics believe that there are always logical, non-ESP explanations behind every apparent case of precognition. For example, in the case of John Godley, skeptics have argued that because Godley was an experienced gambler, he would have had enough knowledge to pick the winning horses himself, conveying his guesses from his subconscious to his conscious mind through dreams. In the case of plane-crash predictions, statistics indicate that a plane crash of some kind occurs at least once a month; therefore if someone predicts a crash without providing many details, the odds are high that the prediction will appear to come true.

But skeptics are not the only ones who have problems accepting the concept of precognition. Even some people who believe in ESP find it difficult to contemplate the idea that the future can be predicted. As Gittelson points out:

While it may be fun to marvel at wondrous precognitive feats, our logical minds are inclined, deep inside, to balk: Precognition can be very fearful to contemplate. Accepting the existence of precognition means accepting that our current concept of time needs radical adjustment.[37]

Chapter 4

How State of Mind Affects ESP

Many cases of telepathy, clairvoyance, and precognition occur while the experient is in the dreaming state. Researchers have considered whether other altered states of consciousness, or ASCs, can enhance ESP, as well as whether people's attitudes and personalities can affect their ESP ability.

ASCs

Drugs, meditation, and hypnosis can all produce an ASC, and all have been studied in connection with ESP with varying results. According to H. J. Irwin, in *An Introduction to Parapsychology*, drug use neither enhances nor hinders ESP ability. Meditation, though, does seem to affect ESP—but not always for the better. For some people, meditation appears to make it easier for them to receive information via ESP, but for others it makes reception more difficult. In other words, while in a meditative state, people either score far better on ESP tests than they do while in a normal waking state or they perform far worse.

The influence of hypnosis on ESP ability is far more difficult to determine. Hypnosis is a seemingly trance-like condition that apparently enhances a person's memory, diminishes the sensation of pain, and leaves the mind open to suggestions made by others. However, psychiatrists disagree on whether it is a real altered state of conciousness. Some believe that hypnosis is not an induced state but the result of normal brain functions. Reporter Roger Highfield discusses both sides of the issue:

> Most scientists now reject the traditional view of hypnosis as a special condition of the brain that is manifested in a sleep-like state, or trance. . . . Some theorists still see hypnosis as an "altered state" which can produce changes in perception and behaviour not capable of being induced by "normal" human processes. But others argue that the phenomena associated with hypnosis can be explained in terms of ordinary human psychological processes such as imagination and relaxation.[38]

Apparently, though, hypnosis slightly enhances ESP ability. But it is also possible that what is improving ESP ability is not really the hypnotic state but the susceptibility to suggestion that is associated with it. A person under hypnosis will generally believe what other people say to believe. Consequently a person being tested for ESP is likely to be susceptible to the beliefs of the researchers conducting the tests—and ESP researchers usually believe not only in the existence of ESP but in the test subject's ESP ability. As Irwin reports: "ESP performance may be enhanced by virtue of the fact that while in one of these states of consciousness the individual is more inclined to believe that ESP is possible; the state of consciousness thus may help to break down or suspend the subject's socially-conditioned intellectual defenses against the notion of ESP."[39]

Under hypnosis a woman raises objects off a table. Great debate exists about the effects of hypnosis and other altered states of consciousness on ESP.

Attitude

This suggests that the key component in doing well on ESP tests is attitude. However, this theory is difficult to study. Irwin explains why:

> [Recent research] indicates that "attitude to ESP" is more complex than one at first might think. "Do I believe in ESP?" may subsume many distinct attitudes and beliefs, including "Would I like ESP to exist?" "Do I think I have ESP?" "Do I think I will exhibit ESP in this particular experiment?" "Do I think this ESP experiment will work (for people in general)?" and "Do I think this experimenter can elicit my ESP?"[40]

The earliest studies related to attitude and ESP focused on the basic question "Do I believe that ESP is a real phenomenon?" Among the first of these studies was one conducted by parapsychologist Gertrude Schmeidler in the

An ESP test is administered to twins. Researchers have tried to determine if the results of ESP tests are affected by the attitudes of the individuals being tested.

1950s. Schmeidler conducted a series of typical ESP tests, but she divided her test subjects into two groups according to whether or not they believed that ESP was real. One group, designated the "sheep," believed in ESP, while the other group, designated the "goats," did not believe in it. Overall, sheep performed better than chance would have predicted on Schmeidler's tests, while goats performed far worse.

In discussing this study, Irwin points out that for the goats to have performed so badly, they had to have been using the very ability—ESP—that they insisted wasn't real:

> The results for goats is most fascinating. Not only does it confirm an effect of attitudes on the occurrence of ESP, it also reminds us of the old adage that there are none so blind as those who will not see. But the fact that goats' mean ESP score is so significantly below chance suggests these people are not merely directing their attention away from extrasensory information nor blocking its cognitive processing; rather they seem to be identifying ESP targets at an extrachance level and then choosing a

different target as their response. By making more incorrect responses than expected by chance, goats seemingly use ESP in a self-defeating endeavor to support their belief that ESP does not exist. It is not that goats are intrinsically insensitive to extrasensory information, but that their attitude affects how they deal with such information.

Irwin adds that Schmeidler's study has been duplicated many times by other researchers, calling it "one of the most success-fully replicated relationships in experimental ESP research."[41]

There have also been variations of this study. For example, in the 1980s parapsychologist B. E. Lovitts led test subjects to believe that they were part of a study designed to prove that ESP did not exist. In this case, goats scored far better than sheep, as recounted by Irwin:

> When [Lovitts] disguised an ESP test as a proce-dure for "disproving ESP," the usual scoring pattern was reversed, that is, sheep tended to perform below chance and goats showed psi-hitting [i.e., correct scores]. This indicates that the sheep-goat effect arises from subjects' use of ESP in confor-mance with their beliefs about it.[42]

Irwin also reports on tests that show that people who fear ESP—usually because they think their minds will be tele-pathically influenced without their consent—score even worse on ESP tests than "goats," who merely don't believe in ESP. People who have neurotic personalities, which means that they spend much of their time in a state of anx-iety, score poorly on ESP tests as well. In contrast, people who have outgoing personalities generally score well.

Mood and Motivation

Not only one's personality but also one's mood at the time of testing also affects ESP scores. In a laboratory setting, mood is measured by having the test subject draw a picture. Someone in a good mood usually draws a much larger, more expansive picture, taking up much more of the page than someone in a bad mood. This phenomenon is called graphic expansiveness. In several studies, people who displayed graphic expansiveness—that is, who were in a good mood—scored better on ESP tests that measured clairvoyance than did people who did not display graphic expansiveness. However, with ESP tests designed to measure telepathy, the reverse was true; people who displayed graphic expansiveness scored significantly worse than those who did not. Researchers are unclear why this disparity exists.

In addition to studies of how attitudes, beliefs, personality, and mood affect ESP test scores, parapsychologists have examined whether a person can be forced to perform well on ESP tests. In the 1950s they conducted a series of ESP tests in which any person giving an incorrect answer was shocked with a mild jolt of electricity; they found that the number of correct answers increased significantly when this was done. However, the study has not been verified by modern researchers, who believe it to be too cruel to perform again.

Other incentives have been tested for their effects on ESP performance. In the 1970s another series of tests examined whether ESP test scores could be improved by offering someone money for every correct answer. They could not. Praising a test subject also does not seem to influence that person's performance.

Imagination

While there is little evidence that people can be motivated to do better on ESP tests, there is ample evidence that people with better-than-average intelligence and good long-term memories perform better on such tests. People who dream vividly and remember those dreams easily also seem to have higher ESP ability. Some researchers believe that high creativity correlates with high ESP ability as well.

Skeptics have interpreted the connection between intelligence, memory, creativity, and ESP to mean that people who seem to have ESP are merely very imaginative and have invented their ESP experiences, either consciously or subconsciously. To skeptics, good ESP results in the laboratory are due to luck; spontaneous incidents of ESP are due to imagination, fantasy, and/or the desire to tell a good story. This is particularly true in cases of spontaneous ESP involving "spirit guides."

Many psychics who receive telepathic messages claim that these messages come not from a living person but from the spirit of a dead one. For example, psychic Sylvia Brown says that she receives much of her information from

Gerry Bowman claims that he channels the spirit of John the Baptist. Psychics who believe they are taken over by a spirit who wants to communicate to the living are called mediums.

the spirit of an Aztec-Incan woman named Francine. To communicate with Francine, Brown puts herself into an ASC—a trance—and while in this state she is "taken over" by Francine's spirit. Francine then uses Brown's body to answer questions posed by people seeking information about their past, present, or future.

Psychics who claim that spirits sometimes take over their bodies in order to communicate are called *mediums*, because they act as the "medium" by which the living can talk to the dead. Those whose spirits primarily lecture and teach in order to impart "ancient wisdom," as opposed to merely answering questions, are called *channelers*. Some psychics, like Brown, are both mediums and channelers because their spirits perform both functions. Others are exclusively one or the other. The most famous channeler is J. Z. Knight, who claims that her spirit guide is Ramtha, a thirty-five thousand-year-old warrior from the Lost City of Atlantis. Thousands of people pay hundreds of dollars to attend Knight's seminars, during which "Ramtha" offers advice. Knight also currently has her own school, the Ramtha School of Enlightenment, which attracts three thousand students for each half-year session.

Mike Dash, in his book *Borderlands*, points out that it is impossible to separate information that might come from the spirit world from information that might come from the imagination, saying that one cannot easily "draw the line between cases that may involve contact with an external intelligence, and those that may be the product of the medium's own mind." He points out that both mediums and channelers do not typically claim to be contacting the spirits of ordinary people. Instead their spirits are usually "wise old American Indians" or "ancient Atlantaens or, in one extreme case, the plastic essence of Barbie (her first message was 'I need respect')."[43] In other words, their spirits are extremely intelligent and/or unusual. Skeptics suggest this is because mediums and channelers have invented their spirits out of a desire to feel special—or, in some cases, because of a mental illness.

In fact, some cases of mediumship have been proven to have been caused by a mental illness known as multiple personality disorder. People with this illness have more than one personality, each with a different name. When one personality is "in control" of the body, the other(s) are "unconscious" and therefore unaware of what the controlling personality is doing. This is similar to the "trance" that the medium or channeler falls into when the "spirit" takes over his or her body.

Spirits or Telepathy?

There is also no way to know whether mediums are truly receiving their information from the spirit world or instead from relatives of the deceased, as Dash explains:

The problem with all such communications [i.e., spirit communications], as psychical researchers have been quick to recognise, lies in the difficulty of excluding any possibility that the information could not have been obtained from a living source by some form of extrasensory perception. Even if outright fraud can be dismissed, all the information in such messages is generally known to the sitter [the person questioning the 'spirit'], at least, and often to friends and relatives as well. It is, thus, at least possible to argue that the medium is obtaining his or her information not from the spirit world, but telepathically, by reading the sitter's mind. This is known as the 'Super-ESP' theory, and it constitutes the principal barrier to the recognition of . . . proof of [the spirit's] survival [after death].[44]

Super-ESP might also be responsible for cases where someone claims to remember living a past life. One example of such a case occurred in 1926, when three-year-old Jagdish Chandra of India told his father and several witnesses that he was once a man named Jai Gopal, who had lived and died in a city three thousand miles away. Chandra provided many details about his former life that were later verified, and when he was taken to meet Gopal's relatives, he pointed the way to their house even though he had never been there before. Similarly, in 1958 two-year-old Gnanatilleka of Sri Lanka described her life as a boy in a nearby village, and when she was taken to meet her former relatives, she was immediately able to identify them. By age seven, however, Gnanatilleka had forgotten her previous life.

The cases of Jagdish Chandra and Gnanatilleka were investigated by Dr. Ian Stevenson, a parapsychologist at the University of Virginia. After studying dozens of past-life experiences, he concluded that the two lives involved in the experience are usually of the same culture and live no further than a hundred miles from one another. Since proximity appears to strengthen ESP and vast distances appear to hinder it, this lends support to the idea that past-life memories are really caused by telepathically communicated information. However, Stevenson himself disagrees with this theory, because the child claiming to have led a past life not only knows information about that life but also behaves similarly to the person who lived that former life. Moreover, other researchers have argued that ESP does not explain why a child would have information on only one other person's life rather than on many people's lives. For example, David H. Lund, in his book *Death and Consciousness*, says:

> If the child is receiving the information via ESP, then why does he identify himself with a certain deceased person? And why does the information that he allegedly acquires by means of ESP seem to be limited to what that deceased person would have known? Why does he have ostensible memories of the life of only *that* person and not others?[45]

Out-of-Body Experiences

Experts also disagree on whether ESP is responsible for another paranormal phenomenon: the out-of-body experience, or OBE. An OBE occurs when—according to experients—the spirit has left the body, allowing the experient to "travel" to a place distant from the body and/or "see" things from a different perspective apart from the body. Dash describes the characteristics of this experience:

> OBEs tend to have several identifiable stages. Typically, the witness suddenly and unexpectedly finds himself "outside" his physical body, perhaps looking down on it from a vantage point near the

ceiling. . . . At this point about half the witnesses become aware that they are now inhabiting a second body, which resembles their own. . . . Now, and with little effort, many witnesses report that they are able to move about at will. They generally perceive the world as solid and realistic—if anything, it seems clearer, brighter and altogether more vivid than usual—and they may be able to visit distant places practically instantaneously. While all this is happening, those who are with the witness report that the physical body remains still and that the subject appears to be in some sort of trance state.[46]

Self-Delusion and Fraud

As with mediumship, some researchers believe that the presence of a trance—an ASC—at the time of the experience is a clear indication that ESP is at work. The connection between altered states and ESP appears strong. However, once again it is difficult to determine whether the phenomenon is due to ESP ability or to imagination, or perhaps to some other cause. Tests of OBEs cannot determine whether "spirit travel" or telepathy or something else is involved.

Such tests typically require a test subject to report something they have "seen" in a distant place to researchers after the OBE is over. For example, in one case a subject "traveled spiritually" to a distant place and "returned" to recite a five-digit number that had been written there. However, as with other ESP tests, skeptics have argued that such tests are inconclusive because there is no way to prove that the test subject did not find out the information in advance. Skeptic James Randi, a former magician dedicated to discrediting, or debunking, all ESP studies, says in his book *Flim-Flam!:*

James Randi, a former magician, spends his time trying to discredit ESP studies.

As I travel around lecturing about so-called paranormal powers and events, I am often confronted with the remark that "scientists have looked into this subject and established its validity." To this I reply by quoting Leon Jaroff, a senior editor of *Time* magazine, who has said, "There has not been a single properly designed, properly conducted experiment that has proven the existence of any paranormal power." I endorse that statement fully.[47]

In considering how state of mind affects ESP, mediumship, and other paranormal phenomena, Randi argues that self-delusion and the desire to defraud are the most common attitudes at work. As an example of self-delusion, he cites an elaborate hoax that he devised in the 1980s to disprove channelers' claims. Through a variety of ruses, Randi convinced the Australian media that a young man named Jose Alvarez—who had no psychic powers whatsoever—was a famous South American channeler whose body was often taken over by "Carlos," a two-thousand-year-old spirit from Venezuela. After the media reported on Jose's amazing ability, people flocked to his public appearances. They also accepted Carlos's intentionally meaningless advice and predictions as valuable, and offered to pay thousands of dollars for some crystals he claimed would heal vague aches and pains. Even after the hoax was revealed, many people continued to express belief in "Carlos." In an interview with John Stossel, Jose Alvarez said: "At the end, there were people saying, 'We know everything they're saying about you. We don't care. We believe in you.'"[48]

In addition to showing how the public can deceive itself regarding psychic ability, Randi has exposed many cases of fraud related to paranormal phenomena. He believes that most cases of ESP and mediumship involve deceit and argues that most scientists are ill-equipped to uncover it:

Many "men of science" stupidly assume that because they have been trained in the physical sciences or the medical arts, they are capable of flawless judgment in the investigation of alleged psychics. Nothing could be further from the truth. In fact, the more scientifically

James Randi works with two boys, Steve Shaw and Mike Edwards, who claimed they had psychic powers. Randi worked at proving their ability false.

trained a person's mind, the more he or she is apt to be duped by an enterprising performer. A scientist's test tube will not lie; another human being will. Scientists are all the more easily deceived because they think in a logical manner. All my efforts as a professional magician are based on the assumption that my audience thinks logically and can therefore be followed by me if I work on that assumption.[49]

Randi and other skeptics seek hard physical proof of ESP—a difficult thing to produce, given that ESP is a mental phenomenon. Tests related to attitude, personality, mood, and other qualities commonly shared by ESP experients are much easier to design, but of course they do not validate whether these experients truly do have ESP or instead share some other cause for their experiences. Consequently some researchers have worked to satisfy skeptics' doubts by exploring possible physical manifestations of ESP in an attempt to prove that it really does exist.

Chapter 5

The ESP-Psychokinesis Connection

Telepathy, clairvoyance, and precognition—if they exist—are mental powers that involve the receipt of information. They affect knowledge but not the physical world, which is why they are so hard to confirm through research. Some mental abilities, however, do appear to influence physical reality. While they are not classified as ESP, like ESP they fall into the broader category of psychic phenomena (psi) and therefore might offer proof that ESP exists. If the mind can influence matter, the argument goes, then surely it can influence other minds.

Ordinary Events

Mental powers that seem to affect the physical world are examples of *psychokinesis*, a word that means "mental movement." There are several types of psychokinesis, or PK. The most basic is the apparent ability to move, bend, or otherwise physically alter inanimate objects using mental effort alone. This alteration can either be mild or dramatic. In discussing the former, Bernard Gittelson explains that many cases of PK are far from memorable. Moreover, people usually explain them away. As an example, he says:

Suppose a teakettle pops off your stove and seems to hover in the air before crashing to the floor. You may be momentarily stunned, but chances are the incident will soon be forgotten, since it's only "something strange" that happened once. If you do continue thinking about it, you'll probably distort your original perception of the event by insisting on a "natural" explanation for it. "Perhaps there was a small seismic disturbance," you might speculate. "Perhaps the teakettle didn't actually hang suspended as long as I thought it did." Or you might say to yourself, "I didn't sleep well last night. I must have imagined it."[50]

Other seemingly ordinary events that might be controlled by PK include computer glitches and slot-machine wins in gambling casinos. Some researchers believe that the mind can influence machines under certain conditions. For example, parapsychologist Dean Radin has studied slot-machine payoffs and discovered that they are the highest during times of a full moon. He notes that during a full moon, the earth's magnetic field is subjected to less interference. Therefore he believes that PK is caused by some kind of magnetic energy that benefits from this same lack of interference.

Psychokinesis, the ability to affect the physical world through mental powers, is often doubted. However, some researchers believe that the human mind can affect such devices as slot machines.

Stopped Clocks

Another type of PK event is the stopped clock, which typically occurs in conjunction with a crisis. This connection between tragedy and PK is not uncommon; as with ESP, it appears that trauma increases the chance that PK will occur. In particular, there have been many stories of clocks or watches stopping at the time of someone's death. For example, one man whose brother gave him a watch as a gift reports:

> I took leave from my job and sat up nights to help my sister-in-law during the last two days of my brother's terminal illness. He breathed his last at six-twenty-five in the morning. . . . At about seven-thirty we were sitting around a rush breakfast—my two brothers, the widow and the nurse. . . . Someone asked me . . . [the time], and I took out the pocket watch . . . and . . . it had stopped at the exact minute of his death. I called the attention of those gathered around the table to the phenomenon and in order to show that it was no common occurrence, asked my brother to wind the watch to make sure it had not run down. It was three-quarters wound.[51]

However, the exact cause of such events cannot be identified, as Gittelson notes:

> The sudden stopping of a watch appropriately symbolizes the end of a person's life, and we're irresistibly compelled to draw a causal relationship here. But how was the watch stopped: by the transformed consciousness of the dying brother or by the shocked mind of the brother who owned the watch? A skeptic might say that the watch-owner accidentally slammed his watch against the wall in his shock at the moment of death, but later forgot about it. In other stopped-clock situations, the two parties were separated by thousands of miles, and the surviving clock-owner was not

consciously aware of the death when it happened. Still, the same questions apply: Was it the "spirit" of the dying man or the telepathically informed mind of the survivor that stopped the clock?[52]

There are also cases of mental clock-stopping that occur as the result of conscious effort rather than as a spontaneous event. These cases are generally part of public performances by professional psychics. For example, psychic Uri Geller, an Israeli psychic who first began demonstrating his psi skills in the early 1970s, routinely stops and starts watches on television shows and in front of paying audiences. He also bends keys and spoons. On some occasions he tells television audiences watching at home that his mental efforts have affected their own possessions, and when they check their watches and spoons they find that these things have indeed been altered.

Many people believe that Geller has genuine PK ability, but skeptics are convinced that he is a fraud. For example, skeptics David Marks and Richard Kammann, in their book *The Psychology of the Psychic*, say that "each and every one of [Geller's] allegedly 'paranormal' events is produced by using a childishly simple conjuring trick." They offer several explanations for how Geller might make it appear that he has mentally bent a key:

> There are many ways of making small objects bend: (1) Distract everybody, bend the object manually, conceal the bend, and then reveal the bend to the now attentive onlookers. This is his usual method. The bend is made either by a two-handed tweak, or by levering it in something tough like a belt buckle or the head of another key with a hole in the top. (2) Geller (or an accomplice) pre-stresses the object by bending it many times until it's nearly at breaking point. Later it can be used to dazzle unsuspecting audiences as it bends, appears to melt, or even snaps in two pieces following the slightest pressure from Uri's wiry fingers.

(3) Quite often collections of metal objects (e.g., a bunch of keys or a drawer of cutlery) contain one or more items that are already bent. Geller tells you he'll bend something and, when you examine the whole set of objects carefully, the bent item is found and Uri takes credit. (4) When an object is already bent, Geller will often say that it will continue to bend. He may move the object slowly to enhance the effect, or place it on a flat surface and push down on one end. But many people will believe they can see an object slowly bending purely as a result of Geller's suggestion that it is doing so. (5) Substitute objects already bent for the ones provided.[53]

Psychic Uri Geller is said to have psychokinetic ability and often demonstrates his talent by bending objects with his mind. Here, Geller holds a fork that he was observed bending while holding it with only one hand.

Marks and Kammann also note that Geller never attempts to bend large objects, only small ones, and never wood objects, only metal ones. They find this significant because small objects are easily manipulated by any stage magician, and, unlike wooden objects, metal objects do not break with a loud snap.

Mediums and PK

Accusations of fraud are also common in cases where the inexplicable movement of objects is associated with mediumship. Some mediums, while communicating with spirits, experience changes in their environment. Tables and chairs might rise, for example, or knocking might be heard for no apparent reason. Mediums say that these events are caused by spirits. Many parapsychologists, however, believe that they are caused by the mediums themselves, via PK. But skeptics argue that all instances of apparent PK concerning mediums are the result of trickery.

Indeed, there is a long history of mediums using tricks to create the sounds and movements of "spirits." For example, sisters Kate and Margaret Fox, both under the age of sixteen, gave public and private séances in the late 1840s and early 1850s during which someone or something unseen knocked on a table in response to questions. Three knocks meant "yes" and no raps at all meant "no"; when the Fox sisters recited the alphabet, a knock came whenever they were meant to write down a letter, thereby spelling out words. Many people believed in the Fox sisters' mediumship, but eventually the sisters confessed that they were fakes (although one of them later recanted her confession). At a public demonstration in 1888, the women showed exactly how they had produced the rapping noises by popping their toe and finger joints.

Around this same period, the SPR uncovered many other cases of fraud among mediums whose work involved physical effects. Consequently the public lost confidence in such mediums—a lack of confidence that still exists today. But parapsychologists argue that just because some physical mediums were fakes does not mean they all were. Perhaps some of them truly were affecting their environment not through physical trickery but through mental influence.

The Fox sisters are shown levitating a table during a séance. The sisters held public séances in the late 1840s to demonstrate their mental powers. Eventually, they confessed having faked their powers, although one sister later recanted her confession.

Poltergeists

The same might be true of a related phenomenon known as poltergeist behavior. The word *poltergeist* comes from the German words *poltern*, which means "noisy," and *geist*, which means "spirit." To people who believe in ghosts, poltergeists are spirits that seem intent on causing trouble by making loud noises, moving objects around, and pushing, pinching, and shoving the living. These

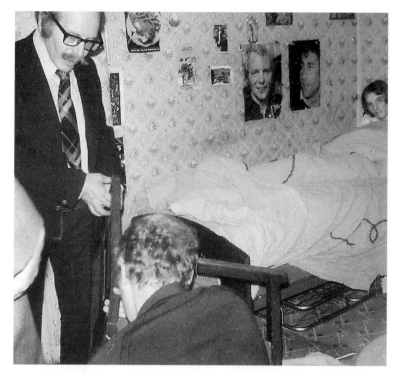

Two investigators examine disturbed furniture in a room, watched by an eleven-year-old girl. The furniture movement was said to be the result of poltergeist activity.

spirits also cause spontaneous, inexplicable fires and strange incidents related to water, such as the appearance in a room of puddles with no apparent cause.

Poltergeist behavior can start suddenly and end suddenly after months or years. Some of this behavior seems tied to a particular place, but in most cases it is related to a particular person. These individuals share certain traits; investigators have found that many of the experients involved in such situations were emotionally troubled adolescents. In one study, approximately 62 percent of experients were under age eighteen and living away from home when the poltergeist activities began. One example of such a case is reported by H. J. Irwin in *An Introduction to Parapsychology:*

> In mid-1965 unexplained movements of merchandise occurred in the chinaware department of a Bremen [Germany] store. Investigations by police and other authorities failed to establish any normal explanation

for the events but they evidently were connected in some obscure way with a 15-year-old apprentice employee in the department. The lad was dismissed and the disturbances in the store immediately came to an end. The young man subsequently obtained a job as an apprentice in a Freiburg [Germany] electrical shop. In March 1966 he was asked to drill holes in a concrete wall and to install wall hooks. The task was done properly but a little later it was found that the hooks came loose in the presence of the young apprentice. He was accused of being to blame. In a test of this a freshly attached hook was observed to come loose within two minutes while the apprentice stood about a yard . . . from the wall.[54]

Because poltergeist experients tend to be under emotional stress, most parapsychologists believe that the physical phenomena that surround these people are due to this stress. In fact, experts suggest that poltergeist experients' unconscious minds might be using PK as a way to relieve emotional tension. Irwin argues that this theory is supported by the fact that most poltergeist activity occurs in the presence of an emotionally troubled teenager, because "it suggests that poltergeist disturbances in some way are associated with emotional conflict in the focal person. The frequency of adolescent cases may indicate further that the [experient] is not in a position to express the conflict openly."[55]

Consequently most experts believe that the term *poltergeist* should not be used to define the behavior at all, since it appears that ghosts are not really involved. For example, parapsychologist William G. Roll says that it is wrong to use a word that means "noisy spirit" because "it implies an agency apart from any living organism." Roll believes that poltergeists are instead a "person-centered phenomenon" caused by recurrent spontaneous psychokinesis (RSPK), which is PK performed both spontaneously and repeatedly.[56]

Laboratory Tests

Skeptics do not believe that RSPK exists, just as they do not believe that PK exists. Trickery is their typical explanation for such events, and they have not been impressed by laboratory tests that seem to support the existence of these phenomena. Many of these tests are similar to tests for telepathy, clairvoyance, and precognition and have similar success rates, with many subjects performing better than chance.

For example, one series of PK studies employed the same machine that Helmut Schmidt designed to test for precognition—a machine that flashes lights in a random pattern. Test subjects were instructed to "will" the machine to create a specific pattern, and in some cases they appeared to be successful in this regard. In another series of tests, a dice-rolling machine was used instead of Schmidt's random-light generator, again with some subjects seeming to influence the roll of the dice at a rate significantly better than chance would have predicted.

As with other ESP laboratory tests involving machines, dice, and cards, there is no way to prove conclusively that these successful results were not due to an unusual run of luck. Therefore parapsychologists have looked for ways to test for PK that do not involve chance at all. For example, in one test in Russia, researchers cracked an egg into a saline solution and required psychic Nina Kulagina to separate its yolk from its white using her mind alone. She did so, although it took over thirty minutes. But she was unable to repeat the experiment, and some Western scientists therefore distrust the test results.

Parapsychologists have also conducted many PK tests related to the mind's effect on plant growth. In one series, each test subject was asked to concentrate on one group of seeds while ignoring another, with the aim of making the first group grow more rapidly. When the growth rate of the two groups was compared over time, the first group did indeed show better progress, and in the end the plants in that group were somewhat taller than the others.

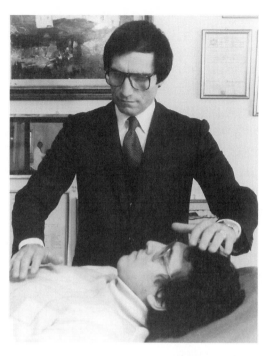

Italian psychic healer Nicola Cutolo treats a patient. Many researchers believe effective healing can happen as a result of patients' own strong desire to get better, not the aid of a psychic.

Psychic Healing

Seemingly successful tests involving the mind's effect on biological organisms such as eggs and seeds rather than on inanimate objects might support the existence of a type of PK known as psychic healing. With psychic healing, an individual claims to have the ability to mentally cure another person's illness. Some researchers believe that psychic healers use PK to alter the unhealthy aspects of the sick person's body, thereby effecting the cure.

However, other researchers believe that the cure is effected by the patient's own mind. There is ample evidence that individuals can alter their own heart rate, blood pressure, and immune systems using mental techniques such as meditation. There is also ample evidence that some people who are physically ill can make themselves well simply by believing themselves to be well. Given that one's mind has such power over one's body, there is no way to be sure that a psychic healing is caused by the healer rather than the healed.

Consequently some scientists have decided that tests using psychic healers and human patients are invalid; they use animal patients instead. In one study, for example, two groups of mice with tumors of identical size were placed in separate cages. Ten times per week for several weeks, a psychic healer concentrated on slowing tumor growth in just one of the groups. By the end of the study, the group "treated" by the psychic healer did indeed have significantly smaller tumors.

Photographic Evidence

In studying the effect of mental energy on animals, plants, and objects, scientists have discovered that all things are surrounded by an electrical field. Using special techniques, images of these electrical fields can be captured through a process known as Kirlian photography. Sheila Ostrander and Lynn Schroeder offer a description of this process in their *Handbook of Psi Discoveries:*

> The most basic Kirlian technique uses a Tesla Coil [an electrical coil] connected to a metal plate. Film and object to be photographed are placed on the plate in the dark. Switching on the current of high-frequency electricity causes the film to record an image of the object including a field around it. Nonliving things such as a coin give a constant unvarying picture, but living things have continuously changing patterns.[57]

The fingers of most healthy humans, for example, are surrounded by a blue-and-white field, while the forearm is typically greenish blue and the thigh olive green. When people are upset, however, these areas all become reddish. Tumors often photograph as gray.

Shortly after the discovery of these energy fields, researchers decided to see whether they could be affected

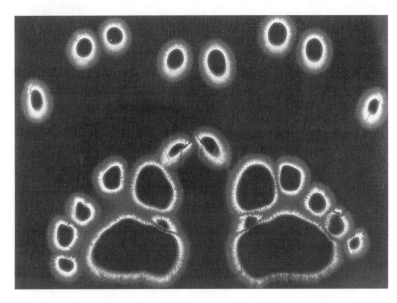

A Kirlian picture of fingers and toes shows the energy fields surrounding the body parts.

by psychic abilities. They discovered that psychics in a trance give off a much brighter, larger energy field than psychics in a normal waking state. They also discovered that psychic healers seem to affect the energy fields of their patients. For example, Professor Douglas Dean, a New York electrophysiologist and parapsychologist, used Kirlian photography to view the energy field of psychic healer Ethel DeLoach. According to Ostrander and Schroeder:

> Mrs. DeLoach had her index finger photographed while resting. It showed average flares. Next she was asked to think about healing. The flare patterns in these pictures showed a large shower of flares pouring from her finger. Each time the sequence was repeated, the same increase in flares showed up. . . . In color photos these flares are predominantly bluish.[58]

Photography has also been used in attempts to document other types of PK. For example, in the 1970s psychic Ted Serios demonstrated an ability to mentally produce images on ordinary photographic plates under the supervision of psychiatrist Jule Eisenbud. According to Irwin, the results of his efforts were impressive:

> The typical procedure . . . was that Einsenbud would point the camera toward Serios and press the shutter release at the moment signaled by Serios. In some sessions Serios was permitted to hold a small tube in front of the camera lens; this so-called "gismo" became the target of criticism by skeptics . . . but even without the device, apparently paranormal effects on the film were obtained. These images included completely black or completely white photographs; fuzzy shadows and silhouettes; and pictures of varying clarity, some of which were of specifically identifiable objects. On many occasions Serios was asked to produce a photographic image of a target defined by the experimenter; some of the resulting prints bear an

Psychic Ted Serios holds the "gismo," a device that aided him in being able to project mental images onto photographic film.

impressive structural resemblance to Serios's mental image of the target.[59]

Ongoing Studies

Other psychics have apparently been able to alter electronic recordings, producing sounds on tape using their minds rather than their voices. This phenomenon was first noticed in the 1950s, but further research into the subject has been scant. However, research into other types of PK as well as into ESP are at an all-time high. Reporter

Kenneth Miller, in a 1998 *Life* magazine article, says that the reason for this lies partly in the fact that skeptics are finding it harder to argue that luck is responsible for all good test results:

> In . . . [his book] *The Conscious Universe*, parapsychologist Dean Radin charted the results of thousands of [ESP and PK] experiments over the past seven decades. Although skeptics claim that hit rates have dwindled as researchers have tightened up their act [i.e., conducted more careful studies], that tendency was nowhere in evidence. In ganzfeld experiments, for example, chance would account for a correct answer 25 percent of the time, yet hit rates averaged 33.2 percent, according to Radin. In psychokinesis experiments, where subjects try to influence either-or events (say, getting a computer-simulated coin-flipper to generate more heads than tails), the margin above chance was narrower but still significant. Taken together, the stats clearly showed that something strange was happening. . . . The question was, was it psi?[60]

No one can be sure whether psi is responsible for successful test results, nor in many cases what kind of psi might be at work. What is clear, however, is that despite the large amount of research already conducted into ESP- and PK-related phenomena, more research is necessary. As the National Research Council stated in 1984 after an extensive study of telepathy, clairvoyance, and psychokinesis: "While the best research is of higher quality than many critics assume, the bulk of the work does not meet the standards necessary to contribute to the knowledge base of science. Definitive conclusions must depend on evidence derived from stronger research designs."[61]

Notes

Introduction: What Is ESP?

1. Mike Dash, *Borderlands: The Ultimate Exploration of the Unknown*. Woodstock, NY: Overlook Press, 2000, p. 95.
2. Theodore Schick Jr. and Lewis Vaughn, *How to Think About Weird Things: Critical Thinking for a New Age*. Mountain View, CA: Mayfield Publishing, 1999, pp. 180, 180–81.

Chapter One: Telepathy

3. Quoted in Bernard Gittelson, *Intangible Evidence*. New York: Simon & Schuster, 1987, pp. 103–104.
4. Gittelson, *Intangible Evidence*, p. 105.
5. Quoted in Richard S. Broughton, *Parapsychology: The Controversial Science*. New York: Ballantine Books, 1991, p. 17.
6. Alfred Douglas, *Extra-Sensory Powers: A Century of Psychical Research*. Woodstock, NY: Overlook Press, 1977, p. 242.
7. Quoted in Gittelson, *Intangible Evidence*, p. 108.
8. Gittelson, *Intangible Evidence*, pp. 107–108.
9. Gittelson, *Intangible Evidence*, p. 108.
10. Quoted in Gittelson, *Intangible Evidence*, p. 109.
11. John Taylor, *Science and the Supernatural*. New York: E. P. Dutton, 1980, p. 58.

Chapter Two: Clairvoyance

12. Dash, *Borderlands*, p. 87.

13. Gittelson, *Intangible Evidence*, p. 111.
14. H. J. Irwin, *An Introduction to Parapsychology*. Jefferson, NC: McFarland, 1989, p. 63.
15. Taylor, *Science and the Supernatural*, pp. 49–50.
16. Douglas, *Extra-Sensory Powers*, p. 337.
17. Joseph McMoneagle, *Mind Trek: Exploring Consciousness, Time, and Space Through Remote Viewing*. Charlottesville, VA: Hampton Roads Publishing, 1997, p. 16.
18. McMoneagle, *Mind Trek*, pp. 62–63.
19. McMoneagle, *Mind Trek*, p. 135.
20. Hans Holzer, *The Directory of Psychics: How to Find, Evaluate, and Communicate with Professional Psychics and Mediums*. Chicago: Contemporary Books, 1995, pp. 7–8.
21. Gittelson, *Intangible Evidence*, p. 118.
22. Quoted in Gittelson, *Intangible Evidence*, p. 119.
23. Sylvia Brown and Antoinette May, *Adventures of a Psychic*. Carlsbad, CA: Hay House, 1998, p. 218.

Chapter Three: Precognition

24. Broughton, *Parapsychology*, p. 8.
25. Schick and Vaughn, *How to Think About Weird Things*, pp. 25–26.
26. Schick and Vaughn, *How to Think About Weird Things*, p. 27.

27. Quoted in Gittelson, *Intangible Evidence*, p. 119.
28. Gittelson, *Intangible Evidence*, p. 121.
29. Gittelson, *Intangible Evidence*, p. 121.
30. Holzer, *The Directory of Psychics*, p. 15.
31. Dash, *Borderlands*, p. 89.
32. Holzer, *The Directory of Psychics*, p. 12.
33. Holzer, *The Directory of Psychics*, p. 13.
34. Dash, *Borderlands*, p. 90.
35. Gittelson, *Intangible Evidence*, p. 123.
36. Holzer, *The Directory of Psychics*, p. 60.
37. Gittelson, *Intangible Evidence*, pp. 125–26.

Chapter Four: How State of Mind Affects ESP

38. Roger Highfield, "The Hypnotic State Remains a Phenomenon That Divides the Experts," *Daily Telegraph*, August 15, 1998.
39. Irwin, *An Introduction to Parapsychology*, p. 95.
40. Irwin, *An Introduction to Parapsychology*, pp. 97–98.
41. Irwin, *An Introduction to Parapsychology*, p. 97.
42. Irwin, *An Introduction to Parapsychology*, p. 98.
43. Dash, *Borderlands*, pp. 84, 84–85.
44. Dash, *Borderlands*, pp. 82–83.
45. David H. Lund, *Death and Consciousness*. Jefferson, NC: McFarland, 1985, p. 165.
46. Dash, *Borderlands*, pp. 96–97.

47. James Randi, *Flim-Flam!: Psychics, ESP, Unicorns, and Other Delusions*. Amherst, NY: Prometheus Books, 1982, p. 2.
48. Quoted in John Stossel (host), *The Power of Belief*, transcript of ABC News special, aired October 6, 1998, p. 13.
49. Randi, *Flim-Flam!*, p. 7.

Chapter Five: The ESP-Psychokinesis Connection

50. Gittelson, *Intangible Evidence*, p. 133.
51. Quoted in Gittelson, *Intangible Evidence*, pp. 133–34.
52. Gittelson, *Intangible Evidence*, p. 134.
53. David Marks and Richard Kammann, *The Psychology of the Psychic*. Buffalo, NY: Prometheus Books, 1980, pp. 112, 115.
54. Irwin, *An Introduction to Parapsychology*, pp. 175–76.
55. Irwin, *An Introduction to Parapsychology*, p. 176.
56. Quoted in Time-Life Books, *Hauntings*. New York: Time-Life Books, 1989, p. 55.
57. Sheila Ostrander and Lynn Schroeder, *Handbook of Psi Discoveries*. New York: Berkley Publishing, 1974, p. 78.
58. Ostrander and Schroeder, *Handbook of Psi Discoveries*, p. 83.
59. Irwin, *An Introduction to Parapsychology*, p. 146.
60. Kenneth Miller, "Psychics: Science or Séance? A Reporter Visits the Twilight Zone," *Life*, June 1, 1998.
61. Quoted in Schick and Vaughn, *How to Think About Weird Things*, p. 182

For Further Reading

Albert Budden, *Psychic Close Encounters*. London: Blandford Press, 2000. This book shares stories of people who have had psychic experiences.

Cassandra Eason, *The Mother Link: Stories of Psychic Bonds Between Mother and Child*. Berkeley, CA: Ulysses Press, 1999. This book shares stories related to telepathic communication between mothers and their children.

Cassandra Eason, *Psychic Suburbia*. London: Foulsham, 1995. This book shares stories about such paranormal events as hauntings and telepathic communication that have occurred among ordinary people in ordinary middle-class neighborhoods.

Fred M. Frohock, *Lives of the Psychics: The Shared Worlds of Science and Mysticism*. Chicago: University of Chicago Press, 2000. This book provides biographical information about famous psychics throughout history, as well as about lesser-known modern ones.

Hans Holzer, *Are You Psychic? Unlocking the Power Within*. Garden City, NY: Avery Publishing, 1997. Although the title of this book suggests that it offers ways for people to test their psychic power, it is actually primarily a collection of stories about people who have had psychic experiences.

Rupert Sheldrake, *Dogs That Know When Their Owners Are Coming Home and Other Unexplained Powers of Animals*. New York: Crown Publishers, 1999. As the title of this book suggests, it concerns ESP in animals.

John Spencer and Anne Spencer, *Powers of the Mind*. New York: TV Books, 1999. This book discusses the latest research on ESP, psychokinesis, spiritual healing, and similar topics.

John Sutton, *Psychic Pets: Supernatural True Stories of Paranormal Animals*. Hillsboro, OR: Beyond Worlds Publishing, 1998. This book for young readers offers stories related to the psychic powers of household pets, including a collie who seems to see ghosts and a psychic who "talks" to horses.

Works Consulted

Richard S. Broughton, *Parapsychology: The Controversial Science*. New York: Ballantine Books, 1991. The director of research at the Institute of Parapsychology, Broughton discusses psychic phenomena from the perspective of a believer and offers scientific evidence to support his views.

Sylvia Brown and Antoinette May, *Adventures of a Psychic*. Carlsbad, CA: Hay House, 1998. This book is an autobiography of Sylvia Brown, a well-known clairvoyant and psychic detective.

Paul Chambers, *Paranormal People*. London: Blandford Books, 1998. This book offers interesting information on people who profess to have psychic abilities.

Mike Dash, *Borderlands: The Ultimate Exploration of the Unknown*. Woodstock, NY: Overlook Press, 2000. Written by an expert in paranormal phenomena, this book presents a wide range of information on current research related to the paranormal.

Alfred Douglas, *Extra-Sensory Powers: A Century of Psychical Research*. Woodstock, NY: Overlook Press, 1977. This book traces the history of psychic research from the 1870s to the 1970s.

Bernard Gittelson, *Intangible Evidence*. New York: Simon & Schuster, 1987. This book reports on research into psychic phenomena and offers tips on how ordinary people can increase their own psychic abilities.

Roger Highfield, "The Hypnotic State Remains a Phenomenon That Divides the Experts," *Daily Telegraph*, August 15, 1998. This article discusses controversies related to the nature and use of hypnosis.

Hans Holzer, *The Directory of Psychics: How to Find, Evaluate, and Communicate with Professional Psychics and Mediums*. Chicago: Contemporary Books, 1995. A noted expert on the paranormal, Holzer categorizes psychics and offers information on how ordinary people can benefit from their abilities.

H. J. Irwin, *An Introduction to Parapsychology*. Jefferson, NC: McFarland 1989. This textbook for advanced readers offers an overview of research into issues related to parapsychology.

David H. Lund, *Death and Consciousness*. Jefferson, NC: McFarland, 1985. This book discusses research related to the conscious mind at the point of death.

David Marks and Richard Kammann, *The Psychology of the Psychic*. Buffalo, NY: Prometheus Books, 1980. Written by skeptics, this book for advanced readers criticizes many aspects of psychic research.

Joseph McMoneagle, *Mind Trek: Exploring Consciousness, Time, and Space Through*

Remote Viewing. Charlottesville, VA: Hampton Roads Publishing, 1997. Written by a participant in the American government's remote-viewing experiments, this book provides detailed information on remote-viewing testing procedures.

Kenneth Miller, "Psychics: Science or Séance? A Reporter Visits the Twilight Zone," *Life*, June 1, 1998. The article reports on the current state of psychic research.

Sheila Ostrander and Lynn Schroeder, *Handbook of Psi Discoveries*. New York: Berkley Publishing, 1974. The main emphasis of this book is Kirlian photography and other physical evidence of psychic ability.

James Randi, *Flim-Flam!: Psychics, ESP, Unicorns, and Other Delusions*. Amherst, NY: Prometheus Books, 1982. Written by one of the most famous skeptics in America, this book criticizes psychics and ESP research.

Theodore Schick Jr. and Lewis Vaughn, *How to Think About Weird Things: Critical Thinking for a New Age*. Mountain View, CA: Mayfield Publishing, 1999. This book encourages readers to question scientific data and consider all sides of issues related to the paranormal.

John Stossel (host), *The Power of Belief*, transcript of ABC News special, aired October 6, 1998. This hour-long television program attempts to debunk a variety of claims related to paranormal phenomena.

John Taylor, *Science and the Supernatural*. New York: E. P. Dutton, 1980. Written by a physicist and mathematician, this book discusses scientific research into various types of ESP and PK.

Time-Life Books, *Hauntings*. New York: Time-Life Books, 1989. This book discusses ghosts and poltergeists.

Colin Wilson, *The Psychic Detectives: Paranormal Crime Detection, Telepathy, and Psychic Archaeology*. San Francisco: Mercury House, 1985. This book provides detailed information on clairvoyance and telepathy as they relate to the work of psychic detectives.

Index

altered states of consciousness (ASCs), 57–58, 63,
67
Alvarez, Jose, 69
animals, 32–33
Apollo 14 mission, 19–20
attitude, 59–61

Borderlands (Dash), 10,
27, 48, 64
Broughton, Richard,
42–43
Brown, Sylvia, 40–41, 63

Cadoret, Remi, 32–33
Carlos, 69
Central Premonitions
Registry, 47
Chandra, Jagdish, 65
channelers, 63–64, 69
Chris (dog), 32–33
Churchill, Sir Winston,
45–46
clairaudience, 40–41
clairsentience, 40–41
clairvoyance
by animals, 32–33
described, 9, 18, 25, 27
fraud and, 31–32

graphic expansiveness
and, 62
precognition and, 41
studies of
by Cadoret, 32–33
by Coover, 18
by the Rhines, 29–32
telepathy and, 25–26,
27–29
tests for, 30
touch and, 38–40
clocks, 73–74
Conscious Universe, The
(Radin), 84
Coover, John E., 17–19
Cox, William, 48
creativity, 62–63

Dash, Mike
on characteristics of
OBEs, 66–67
on clairvoyance, 27
on precognition and
behavior, 48
on psychics and their
spirit guides, 64–65
on reliability of predic-
tions, 51–52
on validity of parapsy-

chology, 10
Dean, Douglas, 82
Death and Consciousnes
(Lund), 66
DeLoach, Ethel, 82
Directory of Psychics, The
(Holzer), 38–39
distance
ESP and, 19–20
spontaneous telepathy
and, 20
Douglas, Alfred
on Cadoret study, 33
on Coover study, 18
dreams
ESP ability and, 62
precognition and, 47,
49–50
spontaneous telepathy
and, 16
drugs, 57

Einstein, Albert, 43
Eisenbud, Julie, 82–83
electrical fields, 80–83
energy levels, 20
ESP
described, 9
general, 25–26

public opinion of, 11
see also clairvoyance; pre-
    cognition; telepathy
experients, 47
experimenter effect, 23–25
Extra-Sensory Powers
    (Douglas), 18, 33

Flim-Flam! (Randi),
    67–69
Fox, Kate and Margaret,
    76
Francine, 63
fraud
    clairvoyance and, 31–32
    PK and, 74–76
    in studies, 31–32, 67–70
    telepathy and, 17

ganzfeld tests, 21–22, 84
Garrett, Eileen, 39–40
Geller, Uri, 9, 74–75
general ESP (GESP),
    25–26
Gittelson, Bernard
    on Churchill's anecdote
        concerning precogni-
        tion, 45–46
    on closeness of relation-
        ship beween those
        involved in telepathy,
        13–14
    on experimenter effect,
        23–24
    on LeShan study of psy-
chometry, 39
    on PK events, 71–72
    on relationship between
        telepathy and clairvoy-
        ance, 28–29
    on Schmidt machine,
        54–55
    on stopped clocks,
        73–74
Gnanatilleka, 65
Godley, John, 49–50, 56
Gopal, Jai, 65
graphic expansiveness,
    62
GRILLFLAME. *See*
    STARGATE

Hansel, C. E. M., 31–32
healing by psychics, 80–83
Highfield, Roger, 58
Holzer, Hans
    on precognition and
        proof, 55–56
    reporting of premoni-
        tions, 47–48
    seriousness of inci-
        dents, 51
    symbolism, 50
    on psychometry, 38–39
*How to Think About Weird
    Things* (Schick and
    Vaughn), 11, 43–44
Hurkos, Peter, 8–9, 39
Hurth, Joicey, 12, 14
hypnosis

ESP and, 57, 58
telepathy and, 20–21

imagination
    OBEs and, 66–67
    past lives and, 65–66
    spirit guides and,
        63–65
Intangible Evidence
    (Gittelson), 13–14,
    23–24, 28, 39
intelligence, 62, 63
*Introduction to
    Parapsychology, An*
    (Irwin), 30, 57, 77–78
Irwin, H. J.
    on ESP and
        ASCs, 57, 58
        attitude, 59, 60–61
    on Kirlian photography,
        82–83
    on poltergeists, 77–78
    on tests for clairvoyance,
        30

Jaroff, Leon, 68–69

Kammann, Richard,
    74–75
Kennedy, Robert, 47
Kirlian photography,
    81–83
Knight, J. Z., 64
Kulagina, Nina, 79
Kuleshova, Roza, 38

Laboratories for
Fundamental Research,
36
LeShan, Lawrence, 39–40
Life (magazine), 84
Lincoln, Abraham,
44–45
Lovitts, B. E., 61
Lund, David H., 66

Maimonides Community
Mental Health Center,
21
Marks, David, 74–75
McMoneagle, Joseph,
33–36
meditation, 57, 80
mediums, 63–65, 75–76
memory, 62, 63
Middleton, Lorna, 47
Miller, Kenneth, 84
Mind Science Foundation,
54
*Mind Trek: Exploring
Consciousness, Time, and
Space Through Remote
Viewing* (McMoneagle),
33
Mitchell, E. D., 19–20
mood, 61–62
Morehouse, David, 33
Morris, Robert, 23
motivation, 62
Murray, Gilbert, 16–17

National Research
Council, 84

Ostrander, Sheila
on Kirlian photography,
81, 82
out-of-body experiences
(OBEs), 66–67
outbounders, 34

parapsychology
described, 9
physical world and, 71
validity of, 10–11
*Parapsychology: The
Controversial Science*
(Broughton), 42–43
past lives, 65–66
Pearce, Hubert, 31–32
personality, 61
poltergeists, 76–79
Pratt, J. G., 31–32
precognition
anecdotes about
Churchill, 45–46
Lincoln, 44–45
Titanic, 45
behavior and, 48
clairvoyance and, 41
described, 9, 42–43,
49–50, 53–54
dreams and, 47, 49–50
premonitions, 46–48
proof of, 55–56

reliability of, 51–53
studies of, 48, 53,
54–55
symbolism and, 50–51
theory of relativity and,
43–44
premonitions, 46–48
psychic detectives
clairsentience and,
40–41
described, 37
psychometry and,
38–39
psychic phenomena (psi),
9, 10–11, 71
psychics
ASCs and, 63
described, 8–9
healing by, 80–83
PK and, 74–75
predictions of, 51
as spirit guides, 63–65
*Psychic Warrior: Inside the
CIA's Stargate Program*
(Morehouse), 33
psychokinesis (PK)
clocks and crises,
73–74
described, 9–10, 54, 71
everyday examples of,
71–72
fraud and, 74–76
mediums and, 75–76
poltergeists and, 78

psychic healing, 80–83
psychics and, 74–75
studies of, 84
tests for, 79
Psychology of the Psychic, The (Marks and Kammann), 74–75
psychometry
described, 38–39
studies by LeShan, 39–40

Radin, Dean, 72, 84
Ramtha, 64
Randi, James
on scientists ability to uncover fraud, 69–70
on validity of ESP studies, 67–69
receivers, 17, 22–23
relativity, theory of, 43–44
remote viewing, 33–36
Rhine, Joseph Banks (J. B.), 15
clairvoyance and, 29–32
Zener cards and, 19
Rhine, Louisa
analysis of spontaneous telepathy by, 15–16
clairvoyance and, 29–32
studies of precognition, 53
Zener cards and, 19

Robertson, Morgan, 45
Roll, William G., 78

Schick, Theodore, Jr.
on explanations for psychic phenomena, 11
on precognition and theory of relativity, 43–44
Schmeidler, Gertrude, 59–60, 61
Schmidt, Helmut, 54–55, 79
Science and the Supernatural (Taylor), 25
senders, 17, 23
Serios, Ted, 82–83
sleep
telepathy and, 21
Society for Psychical Research (SPR)
founding of, 16–17
mediums and fraud and, 76
predictions and, 51
sounds, 83
spirit guides, 63–65
Stanford Research Institute (SRI), 33
STARGATE, 33
Stevenson, Ian
fraud in Rhines' test for clairvoyance and, 32

past lives and, 65–66
study of closeness of relationsip between those involved in telepathy by, 12–13
super-ESP, 65

Taylor, John
on fraud in Rhines' clairvoyance test, 31–32
on relationship between telepathy and clairvoyance, 25
telepathy
clairvoyance and, 25–26, 27–29
closeness of relationship beween those involved, 12–14
described, 9, 12
energy level and, 20
fraud and, 17
graphic expansiveness and, 62
hypnosis and, 20–21
intentional, 16
sleep and, 21
spontaneous
analysis of instances of, 14, 15–16
described, 14–15
distance and, 20
dreams and, 16

studies of
  by Coover, 17–19
  involving hypnosis,
    20–21
  by Maimondes
    Community Mental
    Health Center, 21
  by Murray, 16–17
Titan (Robertson), 45
Titanic (ship), 45

touch, 38–40
trances, 67

Ullman, Montague, 24–25
U.S. Army, 33

van der Hurk, Pieter, 8
Vaughn, Alan, 47
Vaughn, Lewis
  on explanations for psy-

chic phenomena, 11
  on precognition and the-
    ory of relativity, 43–44

Zener, Karl, 19
Zener cards
  Cadoret study and, 32–33
  described, 19
  Rhines' study and,
    29–32

Picture Credits

About the Author

Patricia D. Netzley received a bachelor's degree in English from the University of California at Los Angeles (UCLA). After graduation she worked as an editor at the UCLA Medical Center, where she produced hundreds of medical articles, speeches, and pamphlets.

Netzley became a freelance writer in 1986. She is the author of over two dozen books for children and adults, including *The Curse of King Tut* and *UFOs* for Lucent Books. She and her husband, Raymond, live in southern California with their children, Matthew, Sarah, and Jacob.